Enter Ye in at the
Strait Gate

Enter Ye in at the Strait Gate

The Fate of Mankind Foretold

LOUIS A. KELSCH

iUniverse LLC
Bloomington

ENTER YE IN AT THE STRAIT GATE
THE FATE OF MANKIND FORETOLD

iUniverse books may be ordered through booksellers or by contacting:

iUniverse LLC
1663 Liberty Drive
Bloomington, IN 47403
www.iuniverse.com
1-800-Authors (1-800-288-4677)

Because of the dynamic nature of the Internet, any web addresses or links contained in this book may have changed since publication and may no longer be valid. The views expressed in this work are solely those of the author and do not necessarily reflect the views of the publisher, and the publisher hereby disclaims any responsibility for them.

Any people depicted in stock imagery provided by Thinkstock are models, and such images are being used for illustrative purposes only.
Certain stock imagery © Thinkstock.

ISBN: 978-1-4917-0749-4 (sc)
ISBN: 978-1-4917-0750-0 (hc)
ISBN: 978-1-4917-0751-7 (e)

Library of Congress Control Number: 2013916543

Printed in the United States of America.

iUniverse rev. date: 03/06/2014

Table of Contents

Authors Preface

I write this in the enthusiasm of my love and admiration for the Lord Jesus Christ, and in the hope it will benefit my family. By my family I mean my children, my grand children, my great grand children my siblings, and many, many nieces, nephews, cousins and the wonderful in-laws.

Also for sometime I have felt the desire to convey to my friends, and neighbors some of the great teachings of the Church of Jesus Christ of Latter Day Saints (the Church). This book is an attempt to answer this need.

I am deeply concerned for us mortals. The cover page of this book makes reference to language contained in Matthew 7:13-14 which describes a judgmental observation made by the Lord, as He was concluding His great sermon on the mount. When He declared, that the vast majority of mortals would walk a path in life that takes them to destruction. And that only a very few would find the way to salvation. To me this is a sad commentary on our world, and generations of billions of people.

One of the foibles of us mortals is an obsession with the here and the now. It seems, that often times, the press of daily interests is a huge distraction from time to think and ponder. Also most of us have little inclination to be concerned about transparent vagaries such as an invisible God. Our time and effort is usually consumed meeting the needs and agendas of ourselves and others.

Such effort satisfies the "natural man", but does little for the "spiritual man", and tends to diminish the eternal aspect of our souls. This book is an attempt to encourage more attention to the needs of the spiritual man. One may be pleasantly surprised to find how rewarding the care and nurturing of our spiritual self can be!

It is my hope that those who read this book may indeed gain a greater understanding of the doctrine of the Church and perhaps even a desire to become affiliated with it, or perhaps it could prove useful to strengthen an emerging or frail testimony, of an investigator or member of the church.

I hope the book provokes thought. Sometimes "thought", leads to pondering followed by investigation.

The text of this book presents my own views on the teachings of the Church and I am solely responsible for what has been written and the manner in which quotations were used.

I have written generally of basic viewpoints, that I hold, and that I believe to be critical points of doctrine, and have tried in all cases to validate my viewpoints with references to scriptures in the King James version of the Holy Bible. I also make limited reference to modern day scripture as contained in the Book of Mormon and other scripture unique to this dispensation of time, and to the Church.

I have underlined some of the scriptures to bring attention to those specific phrases, that I felt needed emphasizing. Also I have italicized all scriptures and quotes, and used bold print to emphasize a thought.

The chapter on "works", of a necessity crosses many gospel subjects and will therefore make reference to subject matter previously treated in such discussions as, the fall, the atonement, faith, and repentance. However, I understand that a little repetition is considered a great learning tool.

I encourage you to look up the scriptures quoted, especially those that were merely referenced.

The subject presented in each chapter has by no means been exhausted. To the contrary, in my daily studies of the scriptures I frequently find some new passage or thought that would be an excellent addition to this writing; however, I deliberately avoid the temptation to add such findings in order to leave "the thrill of discovery" to you.

Louis (Lou) Kelsch

The Godhead

The first thing that we must consider in this study, is a concept of what God is like and what our relationship is to Him. The true significance of such an understanding is emphasized in the words of the Savior as He prayed, *"and this is life eternal that they might know thee the only true God, and Jesus Christ whom thou has sent"* (John 17:3).

From this statement we understand that one of the prerequisites of eternal life is to know God and His Son Jesus Christ.

In an effort to explain the nature of God, the majority of the Christian churches, through time and councils, have evolved a doctrine that describes God as a spirit only, without body, parts, or passions, and the Godhead as being comprised of three beings, the Father, the Son and the Holy Ghost, but they are one in substance. This explanation of God and the Godhead is extremely vague and creates virtually no plausible concept of what or who Christians are expected to worship. (see note 1 for discussion on the Spirit of God and of man at the end of this chapter).

However in Genesis 1:26, we read a very plain inference by God to His own bodily characteristics, *"And God said let us make man, in our own image, after our likeness"* . . . . and again in Genesis 1:27, we read, *"So God created man in his own image, in the image of God created he him, male and female created he them"*.

Without groping for dubious meanings we glean from these scriptures, in their simplest interpretation, that mankind looks like God.

To further understand our Heavenly Father, let us for just a moment consider His supreme creation whom He has formed in His own image—MAN.

In general analysis we know that man is composed of a skeletal structure of bones that is covered with sinew and flesh. But there is still a more vital part of man, a part that gives life to the structure of flesh and bones. This part is known as "the spirit", and it is this part that leaves our bodies when we die. The body and the spirit together constitute the soul of man.

Jesus, the one perfect man to walk the earth, was born into this world like anyone else, so He too had a body of flesh, bones and spirit. He was active in his ministry only three years when the Jews crucified Him. His body was wrapped in linen and placed in a borrowed tomb. Three days after His death the spirit of Jesus reentered His body, as He had foretold (John 2:19-22), and He arose (Luke 24: 1-9), a resurrected being having everlasting and eternal life.

The events that transpired immediately after Jesus rose from the tomb are rich in explanation of the physical make up and structure of a <u>resurrected, immortal</u> person.

Luke has recorded a momentous meeting that took place after the death of Jesus.

His Apostles had gathered the eighth day in secrecy for fear of the Jews and were discussing, no doubt, with considerable joy, how the tomb was empty, and that Jesus had appeared to some of them and to the women out side of His tomb. And then Luke tells us of a wonderful thing that happened.

"And as they thus spake Jesus himself stood in the midst of them and saith unto them, peace be unto you. But they were terrified and a affrighted, and supposed that they had seen a spirit. And he said unto them, why are ye troubled and why do thoughts arise in your hearts? Behold my hands and my feet, that it is I myself: handle me, and see; for a spirit hath not flesh and bones as ye see me have. And while they yet believed not for joy, and

wondered, he said unto them, have ye here any meat? And they gave him a piece of a broiled fish, and of an honeycomb, and he took it and did eat before them" (Luke 24: 36-43).

That the Apostles and disciples were terrified and frightened when they saw Jesus, is positive evidence that the time of this meeting was after His death, because they supposed that they had seen a spirit. This reaction of the Lord's disciples is a very normal and human one when we realize that they had recently seen their beloved Master die on the cross. Were this not the case, no doubt His appearance would have caused them to feel joy and certainly not fear.

Let us therefore bear in mind that Jesus stood before His Apostles and disciples, a resurrected man, with a body that was everlasting and had eternal life. Then He opened their understandings and taught them that a spirit and a resurrected man are not the same thing at all, *"for a spirit hath not flesh and bones as ye see me have"*, indeed He invited them to satisfy their curiosity through a sense of perception other than their eyes that afterwards they might not think that they had been deceived. He invited them to touch and handle His body. What the eyes refused to believe the touch would only confirm.

The Jesus that stood before them was a resurrected man. Jesus was now the risen Lord, He had claimed His body through the resurrection. The tomb was empty.

Where then is the resurrected and immortal body of Jesus? The answer lies in the scriptures; for as the Apostles and disciples stood and watched Him ascend into Heaven, two men in white, who were angels, appeared to them and said, *"Ye men of Galilee, why stand ye gazing up into Heaven? This same Jesus which is taken up from you into Heaven, shall so come in like manner as ye have seen him go into heaven"* (Acts 1:9-12).

Jesus ascended into heaven with a solid resurrected body and when He appears the second time He most assuredly will appear with the same, immortal, body.

We have no scriptural or logical evidence to indicate that Jesus at this very moment does not have the same identical body that He showed to his Apostles and disciples.

John in his letter to the saints plainly states, *"When Jesus appears we shall be like him, for we shall see him as he is"* (1 John 3:2).

We know then that Jesus, the Son of God and the second member of the Godhead has an immortal body of flesh, bones and spirit.

God the Eternal Father also has an immortal body of flesh, bones and spirit and is a separate personage from the Son.

In speaking to the Hebrews Paul stated that Jesus, *"is in the express image of God"* (Heb 1: 2-3).

The Savior too made pointed reference to His exact identity to the Father, when He declared to Phillip, *"He that hath seen me, hath seen the Father"* (John 14: 9).

Probably the most obvious refutation of the doctrine propagated by modern day Christianity that God and the Son are one substance is the very relationship that exists between them.

For instance, when Jesus prayed in the garden of Gethsemane, in referring to His impending crucifixion, He asked the Father, *"Remove this cup from me; nevertheless not my will but thine be done"* (Luke 22: 42-44).

The evidence in this scripture that the Father and the Son have separate wills is also a significant testimonial to their individuality.

As if in answer to His prayer an angel came to Jesus to strengthen Him and thereby He learned what course lay before Him for his divine Father had sent Him strength to endure and not to withdraw. (see Luke 22: 43).

The Saviors life is a glorious example of painstaking obedience in word and deed to the will of His Father and there are many scriptures that plainly declare the individuality of the Father and the Son. For example, John 8: 17-18, *"It is also written in your law, that the testimony of two men is true. I am one that bear witness of myself and the Father that sent me beareth witness of me"* . . . . , verse 26, *"and I speak to the world those things which I have heard of him"*, and verse 29, ... *"and that I do nothing of myself; but as my Father hath taught me alone; for I do always those things that please him"*. Also in John 5: 19, we read, ... *The Son can do nothing of himself, but what he seeth the Father do: for what things so ever he doeth, these also doeth the Son likewise"*.

To read these scriptures is to learn that the Father and the Son are two different personages, for here again their individuality is evident in the absolute acquiescence of the Son to the will and commandments of the Father.

In many vital tenets of the gospel the Savior demonstrated the pattern of behavior for all sincere followers through His personal example. As we read of His association with the Father we can see another example of righteousness, in perhaps the most important gospel truth in all Christianity that ever was or ever will be . . . . that of obedience!

To declare that Jesus and the Father are the same personage is to attempt to destroy the relationship that exists between them and to make of little effect or to nullify completely this great example of obedience on the part of the Savior. Indeed the Saviors actions could honestly be considered as fraudulent and deceitful if He and the Father are the same person, because the real value of obedience lies in the act whereby one individual having free choice voluntarily submits His will to the will of another. An act that would be impossible if the Father and the Son were the same personage.

It is true that many scriptures quote Jesus as saying that He and the Father are one, and indeed they are. Let us briefly consider such a scripture. In John 17: 20-21 we read, *"Neither pray I for these alone, but for them also which shall believe on me through their word; that they all may be one; as thou Father art in me, and I in thee, that they may also may be one in us; that the world may believe that thou hast sent me".*

Here we read of Jesus asking His Father to bless His disciples and all those who believe on their words, that they will become one with the Father and the Son. If the "oneness" that Jesus speaks of is actually the same kind of "oneness" as attributed to the Godhead by the sectarian faiths, then all who believe in Christ and accept Him as their Savior, can assume that after this life they will lose their "individuality" in the ethereal mass or substance known as God.

Such doctrine not only has no scriptural basis but is repugnant to the intelligence.

The "oneness" of the Godhead as described in the bible is that of purpose and unity, not substance.

Real achievement and perfection is embodied in oneness wherein separate personalities learn to associate in perfect harmony with one another through mutual obedience to law and order.

Contrary then to popular modern day, "Christian belief ", we learn from the bible that the Godhead actually consists of three separate personages, not one, and that two of these personages have immortal bodies of flesh and bone and spirit while the third is a personage of spirit, *"For he dwelleth with you, and shall be in you"* (John 14:17).

The Latter Day Saints teach and believe that the Godhead consists of three separate personages who are one in purpose and unity, but not substance.

The Latter Day Saint understanding of the Godhead is not derived wholly from the King James version of the bible, but from a marvelous experience that a fourteen year old boy had in the spring of 1820. The name of this boy is Joseph Smith Jr. He was one of a family of eleven souls and, at the time of this experience, lived near Manchester, Ontario County, in the state of New York.

In the community in which the Smith family lived there arose an unusual excitement over the subject of religion. Great prosyleting efforts were being exerted by preachers of many Christian faiths, resulting in serious contentions and bad feelings among the various preachers as well as their converts. As Joseph Smith explains it:

"some were contending for the Methodist faith, some for the Presbyterians, and some for the Baptists. Some crying lo here and others, lo there."

Joseph Smith states that he was confused by the conflicting doctrine of these Christian faiths. He wanted to join a church but was dismayed at the different interpretations of the scriptures that each church presented.

In this troubled state of mind he was reading in the bible, one day in James 1: 5-6 which reads, *"If any of you lack wisdom, let him ask of God, that giveth to all men liberally, and upbraideth not and it shall be given him".*

In his own words Joseph Smith exclaims, *"Never did any passage of scripture come with more power to the heart of man than this did at this time to mine. It seemed to enter with great force into every feeling of my heart. I reflected on it again and again, knowing that if any person needed wisdom of God, I did, for how to act I did not know, for the different sects understood the same passage of scripture so differently as to destroy all confidence in settling the question by an appeal to the bible".*

Joseph Smith eventually decided that the only way to learn what Church was true was to do as James directed and ask God. So, in accordance with this decision he went to a secluded grove of trees, near his home, where he knelt down and commenced to offer up the prayer of his heart to know which of all the Churches was true that he might join it.

He had scarcely begun to pray when he was seized upon by some great power that bound his tongue so that he could not speak and seemed as though it would utterly destroy him. He relates, *"But exercising all my power to call upon God to deliver me out of the power of the enemy that had seized upon me, and at the very moment when I was ready to sink to despair and abandon myself to destruction, not to an imaginary ruin, but to a power of some actual being from the unseen world, who had such an astonishing influence over me as to bind my being, just at this moment of great alarm I saw a pillar of light exactly over my head above the brightness of the noon day sun, which descended gradually until it fell upon me. It no sooner appeared than I found myself delivered from the enemy which held me bound. When the light rested upon me I saw two personages, whose brightness and glory defy all description, standing above me in the air. One of them spoke unto me, calling me by name, and said, pointing to the other . . . . This is my beloved Son hear him".*

Joseph's purpose in going to the Lord was to learn which of all the sects was right. He therefore no sooner gained sufficient possession of himself so that he was able to speak, than he asked the personages who stood above him, what church he should join. He was told, *"You must join none of them, for they are all wrong"*, and the personage who addressed him said that: *"all their creeds are an abomination in my sight, for they draw near to me with their lips, but their hearts are far from me, they teach for doctrines the commandments of man, having a form of Godliness, but they deny the power thereof"* (Joseph Smith History 1:1-19).

During this highly significant and glorious interview, Joseph Smith was told that if he were true and faithful in all things he would be an instrument in the hands of the Lord in bringing forth the Church of Jesus Christ.

Joseph didn't go into the grove of trees to get a new Church. He assumed one of the existing ones was the true one, and only wanted to know which one it was.

This revelation was not expected or sought after. However when he came out of the grove of trees he knew beyond a shadow of a doubt that God and His beloved Son, the Lord Jesus Christ, lived.

He learned that each has a glorified body and that they are two distinct and individual beings. He learned that man is indeed created in the image of God, and that Deity will speak to a man or a boy if they choose too. He also learned that these powerful beings had a work for him to do, and his life had just taken a profound and sobering direction.

Joseph went into the grove of trees to make an oral attempt at prayer, perhaps because his home, a small structure was very crowded with 11 souls living in a small space. He had seen this particular grove of trees before and was impressed with the quiet and beauty of the place.

I have been there. The grove is about 2 city blocks from the house he lived in. It is a large grove of poplar trees with a small clearing in the center. I was there, alone, on a cool sunny September morning. Birds were chirping and the floor of the grove was covered with a growing carpet of leaves. The sun was streaming down through the bright autumn leaves. It was very pretty. Who hasn't seen a beautiful view of nature and felt the awe of being in the presence of the majesty of God.

One might think that this was a very mature decision for a fourteen year old boy. But we must remember that frontier teenagers matured fast under the challenge of heavy work. Cutting and clearing trees, stumps and moving rocks, in order to plant and tend a crop to provide food for the family and some meager cash necessities was dawn to dusk labor and all hands were badly needed. Daily life was a serious business usually requiring one to grow up fast. Education was attempted after work around the kitchen table reading the bible by candle light.

Also there is no doubt that Joseph had faith that he would receive an answer. The effort to go to the grove and their to make the attempt to talk with God bears testimony to his faith.

It is also important to remember that at age fourteen, Joseph had not developed the sophistication to settle in his mind the decisions of weighty philosophical matters that most of us establish in our lives, usually at a time when we venture forth on our own.

Said another way, at his tender years, he had very few preconceived notions about life.

His was an unfettered intellect, a clean vessel in which to "pour new wine" (see Luke 5: 36–38).

This dramatic and profound experience, that came to a teen age boy in the frontier of America, was the making of a Prophet of God, in these latter days and the beginning of an original American church.

NOTE 1

The majority of the Christian world maintain that God is a spirit. I believe they derive this position from the scripture, *"God is a Spirit: and they that worship him must worship him in spirit and in truth."* (John 4:24).

Yes God is spirit and much, much more . . . . He is a glorified immortal being, and it is His desire to make the same out of us, if we would just quit resisting Him.

I counted no less than 30 scriptures in the King James version of the bible that speak to the corporeal nature of God, as to His image, His face, His feet, His finger, His back parts, eating mortal food, His form, His appearance, and our resemblance to Him.

In the same sense it can be said that God is a spirit, it can also be said, *"man is spirit"*.

Unquestionably the spirit of man is the life force of the flesh. So yes we too are spirits.

God, is immortal but has the power through His spirit to touch our spirits. Why does God prefer to communicate with us through the spirit, ... either by His own spirit or influence or that of the Holy Ghost?

For one thing, lets be perfectly clear . . . . God can do anything He wants. However He seems to prefer to communicate with us through the spirit as a blessing to us.

Our Spirits are the one component of our soul that is eternal. God sees fit to communicate with that part of us that He is the Father of and that is also eternal . . . . and in so doing by passes the sophistry, and the filters of the flesh.

Perhaps another reason is that our spirit is the part that returns to Him when we die, to await resurrection and judgment.

How does He communicate with us? Again anyway He wants. Most commonly by His spirit, often referred to as "our conscience" as it pertains to the choices in our daily lives, and the answering of our prayers, ... and by the Holy Ghost as the message pertains to understanding and learning the principles of salvation, and again the answering of prayers . . . . or by specific messages from special messengers often referred to as angels.

Apparently the spirit of God is a powerful means of communication, with His children.

Some times we get so caught up in materialism, we don't even make the effort to communicate with God, we forget about Him. In such circumstances God may speak to us in a much more dramatic way to get our attention. He may speak to us with earthquakes, storms, fire, wars, and famines, to bring us into remembrance, and remind us who we are.

The Great Apostasy

During his extraordinary interview with the Father and the Son, Joseph Smith was told that he was to join none of the churches, because they were all wrong. They had a form of Godliness but denied the power thereof.

In this chapter we will consider the reasons why the Lord said what He did about the Christian Sects of today. This review will take us back through the years to ancient Jerusalem in the days when Jesus walked on the earth and preached the principles of salvation to all who would listen.

In those days, just as today, there were a number of different religious sects in existence built around pagan deities. However, Jesus accepted none of them but established His own Church. One of the first things He did in organizing His Church was to call and ordain twelve Apostles with power and authority to act for God in His name (see Matt 10:1, and Luke 6:13).

The selection of the twelve Apostles was of vast importance to Jesus. Whoever was chosen would be called upon to bear the spiritual and temporal responsibility of His Church after His death. Jesus spent the entire night in prayer to God, before the day on which He selected His Apostles (see Luke 6:12). On the following morn He called His disciples together and from them He chose twelve whom He named Apostles.

We cannot question that the Apostles prior to their ordination, had a strong desire to serve the Lord; several, had given up all they had to follow Him. Nonetheless Jesus made it clear to them that their heart felt desires alone, although necessary, did not make them authoritative ministers when He instructed them, *"Ye have not chosen me but I have chosen you and ordained you"* (see John 15:16).

Upon receipt of the authority or priesthood to act for God, the twelve Apostles received powers they had not possessed as disciples. Powers over unclean spirits, power to heal all manner of sickness and disease, power to seal on earth and whatsoever was sealed on earth would be sealed in Heaven, and whatsoever was loosed on earth would be loosed in Heaven (see Matt 18:18).

And with this power came proselyting responsibilities to preach at first, only to the Jews, *"the lost sheep of the house of Israel"* (Matt 10:5-6), and their message was to be, *"the kingdom of God is at hand."* (Matt 10:7).

Later the resurrected Lord said to the Apostles: *"Go ye into all the world and preach the Gospel to every creature. He that believeth and is baptized shall be saved but he that believeth not shall be damned."* (Mark 16:15-18).

Inherent with the powers they had been given, the Apostles also received authority to baptize. Indeed in accordance with the scripture just quoted in Mark, baptism is essential to salvation.

We can further appreciate the care that Jesus took in selecting the twelve Apostles and in giving them the authority, or priesthood, when we realize their position in His Church.

Paul pointed out this relationship in his epistle to the Ephesians when he declared, *"Now therefore ye are no more strangers and foreigners, but fellow citizens with the saints and of the household of God; and are built upon the foundation of the Apostles and Prophets, Jesus Christ Himself being the chief cornerstone; in whom all the building fitly framed together growth unto an holy temple in the Lord; in whom*

15

ye also are builded together for an habitation of God through the spirit." (Eph 2:19-22).

In writing to this gentile flock, Paul told them that they were now just as privileged as the Jews to hear the gospel of Jesus Christ, and were therefore *"no more strangers and Foreigners"*, but were indeed *"fellow citizens with the saints"*, and just as much of the *"household of God"*, as were the Jews.

Paul likened the church of which they were now part, unto a fitly framed building and declared that the foundation of the building was the twelve Apostles, and Jesus, who had ascended to Heaven, was the chief cornerstone. The cornerstone of any building is the part of the foundation to which the rest of the foundation is perfectly aligned and made true so that the building will be level and dimensionally true as it is framed . . . . so that it will be <u>fitly framed.</u>

And the Apostles were the very foundation of this building, or organization. And why were the Apostles designated as the foundation? Because they had been given the authority to act for God, and that authority is called Priesthood. And the name of that Priesthood is, the very same that Jesus held, ... the Holy Priesthood *"after the order of Melchizedek"* (see Hebrews 5:1-10).

Every one knows that a building cannot stand without a foundation, by the same token a foundation does not constitute a completed building. So even though the Apostles were unquestionably of vast importance to the Lords organization other offices were required as well. Paul refers to other offices in his epistle to the Ephesians, thusly:

"and he gave some, <u>apostles</u> and <u>prophets</u>; and some <u>evangelists</u>; and some <u>pastors</u> and <u>teachers,</u> for the perfecting of the saints, for the work of the ministry, for the edifying of the body of Christ; Till we all come in the

unity of the faith, and of the knowledge of the Son of God, unto a perfect man, unto the measure of the stature of the fullness of Christ; That we henceforth be no more children, tossed to and fro, and carried about with every wind of doctrine by the slight of man and cunning craftiness, whereby they lie in wait to deceive" (Eph 4:11-14).

Other priesthood offices that also existed in the Lords church besides those mentioned by Paul, in his epistles, are *"High Priests"* (Heb 5:1), *"Elders"* (1 Tim 5: 17), *"Seventies"* (Luke 10:1), *"Bishops"* (1 Tim 3:1), *"Priests"* (Luke 1:5), and *"Deacons"* (1 Tim 3:8).

In his writings to the Ephesians Paul explained, that Jesus *"gave"*, the Priesthood for the perfecting of the saints and for the work of the ministry.

Consider this scripture, in Ephesians, carefully for herein Paul declared that imperfect saints, through priesthood leadership, inspired by the Holy Ghost can achieve the *"stature of the fullness of Christ"*. And who is Christ? He is a God and occupies a place at the right hand of His divine Father by virtue of the things that He suffered (see Heb 1:1-3).

Paul therefore knew and preached that sinful man, under inspired Melchizedek Priesthood leadership, could become as God. For whosoever achieves the *"stature of the fullness of Christ"*, will be a God, just as Christ is!

After the death and ascension of Jesus to Heaven, He through the Holy Ghost continued to guide and direct the Church He organized through His Apostles. He continued as the head of the Church and directed its affairs, from Heaven by divine revelation through the Holy Ghost to, the *"foundation of the Church"*, the twelve Apostles.

Consider the following scriptures of the new testament as recorded in the Acts of the apostles, and as you read note the position of the Holy Ghost both as an intermediary between the Lord and His anointed servants, and also as an independent authority, providing direction as the third member of the Godhead.

"As they ministered to the Lord and fasted, <u>the Holy Ghost said</u>, separate me Barnabas, and Saul for the work where unto I have called them" (Acts 13:2) *"So they being <u>sent forth by the Holy Ghost,</u> departed unto Seleucia; and from thence they sailed to Cyprus"* (Acts 13:4).

And again a letter from the Apostles to the gentile converts, in Antioch, Syria, and Celicia, stated in part; *"For it seemed good <u>to the Holy Ghost</u> and to us, to lay upon you no greater burden than these necessary things"* (Acts 15:28). To read these scriptures and indeed the entire Acts of the Apostles, is to learn that these men were guided from on high by the Holy Ghost.

Here then begins to appear the evidence of a marvelous truth. The true Church of Jesus Christ must always receive continuous revelation until the Lord, returns to the earth and personally assumes the reins of government. Why is this so one may ask? The answer is simple, ... Jesus is the head of His Church. He directs its affairs from Heaven. The act by which He communicates with His chosen servants is known as revelation, and the agency that conveys such revelation is none other than the Holy Ghost. Therefore it is not strange to read that the Holy Ghost actually directed the Apostles and subsequently the affairs of the Church.

Jesus as He was contemplating His death, instructed and comforted the Apostles thusly; *"It is expedient for you that I go away; for if I go not away, the comforter, will not come unto you; but if I depart, I will send him unto you."* (John 16:7).

And what are some of the functions of the Holy Ghost? *"He shall teach you all things, and bring all things to your remembrance whatsoever I have said unto you"* (John 14: 2-6); *"He will guide you into all truth, for he shall not speak of himself, but whatsoever he shall hear, that shall he speak; and he will show you things to come."* (John 16:13).

Now all this discussion about the Holy Ghost is to further exemplify that the Church of Jesus Christ, in the meridian of time, was guided by revelation from the Lord after His crucifixion and ascension to heaven and not by the will and precepts of well meaning men.

These revelations from God to His chosen Apostles and Prophets were committed to writing and are the scriptures we have today.

We know from previous discussions that the Apostles were the literal foundation of the organization of the Church of Jesus Christ, because they held the true Priesthood and authority, and because they received revelations for the guidance of the church.

Picture in your mind a large building with a foundation of twelve stout pillars. What would happen to that building if the pillars were knocked from beneath it? It would collapse of course, and break to pieces. It would cease to be a fitly framed building. And that is exactly what happened to Christ's Church in the meridian of time. The Apostles were all killed or otherwise done away with and the Church fell.

The fall of the Church is known as "The Great Apostasy", and constitutes the loss of true authority and priesthood to the earth because of the wickedness of man. This "Apostasy" did not transpire over night but actually covered a long period of time. From the scriptures we learn that such an event as this would occur and had actually begun prior to the death of the Apostles.

Paul warned the Elders at Ephesus, *"For I know this, that after my departing shall grievous wolves enter in among you, not sparing the flock. Also of your own selves shall men arise, speaking perverse things to draw away disciples after them"*(Acts 20:29-30). John in his epistle to the saints declared, *"Little children it is the last time; and as ye have heard that anti-Christ shall come, even now are there many anti-Christ; whereby we know that it is the last time. They went out from us, for if they had been of us, they would no doubt have continued with us: but they went out, that they might be made manifest that they were not all of us"* (1 John 2:18-19).

In a letter to the Galatians Paul spoke of those who were trying to pervert the gospel and lead the saints astray and wondered at the lack of faith of the Galatians as he remarked, *"I marvel that ye are so soon removed from him that called you into the grace of Christ unto another gospel; which is not another, but there be some that trouble you, and would pervert the Gospel of Christ. But though we or an angel from Heaven, preach any other gospel unto you than that which we have preached unto you, let him be accursed"* (Galatians 1:6-8).

It was during this time that the Thessalonians fell into error and believed that the day of the second coming of Christ was near at hand, however; Paul declared to them, *"Let no man deceive you by any means; for that day shall not come, excerpt there come <u>a falling away first</u>"* (2 Thess :2-3).

Here the Thessalonians learned that the day of the second coming of Christ would not come until there was first a falling away from the truth.

Jesus knew what would befall His Church and warned His Apostles, *"Yea, the time cometh that whosoever killeth you will think he doeth God service and these things will they do unto you, because they have not known the Father nor me"* (John 16:2-3).

It appears that the death of the Apostles was a foregone conclusion, and they would suffer death at the hands of a wicked and perverse people.

Indeed the scriptures declare that the Church established by Jesus Christ would be perverted by wicked men and the Priesthood driven from the earth by an unrighteous people who knew not the Father nor the Son, *"but after their own lusts shall they heap to themselves teachers, having itching ears; and they shall turn away their ears from the truth and will be turned unto fables"* (2 Tim 4: 3-4).

So as was prophesied the Apostles were all killed or otherwise done away with, the foundation of the Church was swept from beneath it and the true Priesthood of God was withdrawn to Heaven to the source from which it came.

One might then say, well, if the truth and the Priesthood were actually taken from the earth, in what position does that place the hundreds of Christian church's in the world today. If the Priesthood authority continued from Peter as so many believe why aren't these Churches organized and fashioned after the manner established by the Apostles and Prophets of the meridian of time?

If they have no authority because it was taken from the earth how valid are sacraments and ordinances performed by ministers and priests of these churches?

In consideration of these serious questions let us first review generally, the organization of the Catholic and Protestant Churches. Do they have a foundation of twelve Apostles and Prophets? The answer is no! However some will say that the Catholic Church has a comparable foundation in the one-hundred plus Cardinals. Does it really? When Judas betrayed the Lord, he fell from his apostleship, hence, there remained eleven Apostles.

From the scriptures we read of the manner in which this vacancy was filled, *"And they appointed two, Joseph called Barsabas, who was surnamed Justus and Matthias. And they prayed and said, Thou Lord, which knowest the hearts of all men, shew whether of these two thou hast chosen, that he may take part of this ministry and apostleship, from which Judas by transgression fell, that he might go to his own place. And they gave forth their lots; and the lot fell upon Matthias, and he was numbered with the eleven apostles"* (Acts 1 :23-26).

So through revelation the quorum of the twelve Apostles was restored to its full strength. Why didn't they, the eleven, just leave things as they were, or why didn't they call both Barsabas and Matthias to the apostleship and have thirteen apostles?

The apostles sought revelation and they got it, from He who organized the foundation of the church in the first place. And He ordained that there should be twelve apostles, not eleven or thirteen, or one hundred some odd, but twelve.

Do these Churches receive continuous revelation as did the Lords church, as evidenced by the accumulated scripture known as the new testament. The answer is no they do not, and what's more they don't claim to. The Catholic church claims inspirational interpretative powers of existing scripture through the Pope. The Protestant churches not only claim no revelation, but hold with the view that all revelation has been given that is going to be given. These people deny God the power of communication with his own creations.

Is it any wonder Jesus said to the boy Prophet on the American frontier, of these religions, *"they draw near me with their lips, but their hearts are far from me. They have a form of godliness but deny the power thereof"* (Joseph Smith 2:19, see also Matt 15:8-9). Baptism in these Churches establishes the recipients membership in that Church, as an initiation right, and that is well and good if that is what the individual wants. But there is no saving grace associated with that baptism.

Did Christ the only perfect being suffer untold pain and excruciating agony both in the garden of Gethsemane and again on the cross so that all of us can believe anything we want? No! I say with Paul, *"Endeavoring to keep the unity of the spirit in the bond of peace. There is one body and one spirit, even as ye are called in one hope of your calling; One Lord, one faith, one baptism, One God and Father of us all, who is above all, and through all, and in you all"* (Ephesians 4: 3-6).

It is true that many of the ministers of these churches are sincere in their beliefs and practices, so too was Paul as he set about to persecute the saints of God in the meridian of time. And even though Paul was personally convinced that what he did was right, he learned it was wrong when the resurrected Lord spoke from the Heavens and said, *"Saul, Saul, why persecutes thou me"* (Acts 9:4)?

The character trait of sincerity, while helpful, does not in and of itself qualify a man to the ministry of Christ. Neither does college qualify a man for the ministry, but rather, Jesus is the one who decides who will minister in His Church and makes those selections just as He did when He was on the earth. Did He not declare to the twelve, *"Ye have not chosen me <u>but I have chosen you</u> and ordained you"* (John 15:16)?

And after His ascension to heaven, wasn't it the Holy Ghost who issued calls to the ministry through Christ's Apostles and Prophets or those whom they called? This is the method used in the meridian of time in staffing the Lords Church. Is it not only logical that Christ would decide who would minister in <u>His Church?</u>

Baptisms and other ordinances performed in the name of Jesus Christ by unauthorized men are not recognized by Him and are therefore not efficacious to the recipients, as a saving grace.

The Christian churches do not have Apostles and Prophets, they do not have the Melchizedek Priesthood, they do not receive continuous revelation from the Lord and don't claim to and certainly do not have the evidence of any such scripture as would exist in a Church with continuing revelation.

For this reason we can better understand why the Lord said what He did to the Prophet Joseph Smith concerning the churches of this day and age.

Did not the Lord in a revealing moment explain what the spiritual fate of the world would be, as recorded in Matthew 7: 13-14, *"Enter ye in at the strait gate: for wide is the gate, and broad is the way, that leadeth to destruction, and many there be which go in thereat: Because strait is the gate, and narrow is the way, which leadeth unto life, and few there be that find it"*.

From this scripture it would appear that the Lord had just rendered a judgmental observation on the billions of all who are or have been mortals, as to what will happen to them, as a result of the decisions they made in mortality.

So I say to you dear reader, look for the church that is identical to the church Jesus organized in the meridian of time. Find it . . . . its here on earth.

Make the effort to pray. You are Gods off spring, ... talk to Him. Your eternity depends on what you do here and now in mortality. And you really don't have much time. Don't put off until tomorrow, because tomorrow really never comes . . . . it's always today.

The Restoration

From the foregoing chapters we have learned there was no true church on the earth with authority to act for God at the time of the visitation of the Father and the Son to Joseph Smith.

The power to represent deity which had been given to man by the Savior during the meridian of time was virtually driven from the earth by a hard hearted people who sought doctrine that supported their evil and perverted ways, rather than learn the truth and repent.

Amos, an ancient Prophet, saw this great loss to the earth and prophesied thusly; *"Behold, the days come, saith the Lord God, that I will send a famine in the land, not a famine of bread, nor a thirst for water, but of hearing the words of the Lord; And they shall wander from sea to sea, and from the north even to the east, they shall run to and fro to seek the word of the Lord, and shall not find it"* (Amos 8:11-12).

The world experienced a profound spiritual dearth during the time called the Dark Ages.

Obviously it was never the Lords intention to indefinitely withhold the Gospel from generations subsequent to the meridian of time. To do so would put the Lord in the position of being a respecter of persons, since the gospel message is such a rich blessing to any generation, being the only way of salvation.

The Lord has expressly avowed that He is no respecter of persons (see James 2:1-4, and Acts 10:34) and would therefore, certainly love generations yet unborn as much as He loved those of the meridian of time and earlier.

The restoration of the gospel to the earth as an event in the last days was seen and understood by an ancient Prophet, Daniel as he interpreted the dream of King Nebuchadnezzar by revelation from the Lord, ... who was known anciently as Jehovah.

It seems that this king, the ruler of the great Babylonian empire had a dream that really distressed him, in fact he was so disturbed he couldn't sleep. The King called together his magicians, his astrologers, and his sorcerers, and commanded them to interpret his dream. When they inquired of the King what the dream was, the King said, *"The thing is gone from me; if ye will not make known unto me the dream, with the interpretation thereof, ye shall be cut in pieces, and your houses shall be made a dunghill"* (Dan 2: 5).

An interesting response, since unquestionably the King remembered his dream and didn't want to tell his wise men and have them make up some plausible response. He wanted verification that they could perform a supernatural reading, for surely if they could do that they could provide a correct interpretation . . . . clever King!

Naturally the wise men were abashed and said, *"There is not a man upon the earth that can shew the King's matter".* This was the wrong answer . . . . and infuriated the King then commanded all the wise men of the empire to be sought out and slain.

Daniel learned of this "hasty" decree from the Kings captain and declared to the King *"The secret which the King hath demanded cannot the wise men, the astrologers, the magicians, the soothsayers, shew unto the King; but there is a God in Heaven that revealed secrets, and maketh known to King Nebuchadnezzer what shall be in the <u>latter days.</u> Thy dream and the vision of thy head upon thy bed are these"* (Dan 2:27-28).

And then Daniel by revelation from God proceeded to tell the King what he dreamed.

As the story unfolds, as recorded in Daniel 2: 31-35, the King in his dream saw a huge statue or image. The image's head was gold, his breasts and his arms were of silver, his belly and his thighs of brass, his legs of iron, and his feet part of iron and part of clay.

Next the King saw a stone cut out of a mountain, without hands, which smote the image on the feet of iron and clay and brake them to pieces. *"Then was the iron, the clay, the brass, the silver, and the gold, broken to pieces together and became like chaff of the summer threshing floors; and the wind carried them away, that no place was found for them: And the stone that smote the image became a great mountain and filled the whole earth"* (Dan 2:35).

With the explanation of the dream concluded Daniel then proceeded to give the interpretation.

The head of gold of this great image, was none other than King Nebuchadnezzer himself, and his Babylonian empire, the then ruler of the world. The King was told that after him would arise other kingdoms inferior to his and they would rule the world. These kingdoms were represented by the inferior metals of the image; the silver, the brass, the iron and lastly the iron mixed with clay.

Perhaps an explanation of this great image may be better portrayed with the following chart:

IMAGE	RULING KINGS/ POWERS	APPROX. DATES
Head of gold	Babylonian empire	677 BC to 538 BC
Arms & breast of silver	Meado-Persian empire	538 BC to 331 BC
Belly of brass	Greeks (Alexander)	331 BC to 161BC

IMAGE	RULING KINGS/ POWERS	APPROX. DATES
Legs of iron	Roman empire (time of Christ)	161 BC to 433 AD
Feet / toes of iron & clay	10 recognized kingdoms	1830 AD

This image represented the powers that would exercise dominion in the world, from King Nebuchadnezzer's time to the latter days.

Of the kingdoms portrayed by the feet of the image, Daniel said, *"And whereas thou sawest iron mixed with miry clay, they shall mingle themselves with the seed of man; but they shall not cleave one to another, even as iron is not mixed with clay"* (Dan 2:43).

Doesn't this scripture portray the mingling of monarchs in our own day with the common man? Have we not seen come to pass the demise of the great era of absolute monarchism in Europe? And those nations who yet sustain a monarchy do so as a figure head only, the real power of government being invested in the people as represented by parliaments, or congresses.

And yet . . . . it was in the days of the kingdoms represented by the feet of the great image, that Daniel prophesied God would establish His kingdom on the earth: *"And in the days of these Kings shall the God of Heaven set up a Kingdom, which shall never be destroyed ; and the Kingdom shall not be left to other people, but it shall break in pieces and consume all other Kingdoms and it shall stand forever"* (Dan 2: 44).

The Savior established a Church in the meridian of time during the world reign of the Roman Empire, or the legs of iron depicted in the vision of the great image.

However, the Lord revealed through Daniel that the establishment of His permanent Kingdom, one that would never be permitted to be driven from, or taken from the earth, would not occur during the period represented by the kingdom of iron but rather some 1800 years later when the affairs of the Roman Empire were history. What a marvelous vision and how clearly it substantiates the actuality of a restoration.

Peter, the chief Apostle of the Lord, knew that the Church over which he presided would fall and taught it to the people of his day. *"Repent ye therefore, and be converted that your sins may be blotted out, when the times of refreshing shall come from the presence of the Lord; and he shall send Jesus Christ, which before was preached unto you: <u>Whom the Heaven must receive until the times of restitution of all things,</u> which God hath spoken by the mouth of all his holy Prophets since the world began"* (Acts 3:19-21).

Here we may ask, why would Jesus Christ appear to a boy in upstate New York, to inaugurate a restoration of all things, if indeed *"all things",* were already on the earth as they most certainly would be, if the claim of the Catholic and Sectarian Churches were true; wherein, they maintain the Gospel and authority to act for God has never left the earth and has been handed down to succeeding generations from Peter.

If the Catholic and Sectarian Churches of today are right then we must say . . . . Oh Peter you err, ... we need no more restoration, we have everything we need for our salvation without a restitution.

But Peter we know was indeed an ordained Apostle under the hand of Jesus Christ Himself and did not err and did see the necessity of a restoration of all gospel principles, including the Priesthood or authority to act for God, Peter himself being a recipient of that authority. And you will also note from Peters declaration that it would be none other than the Lord Jesus Christ who would "*initiate the restitution of all things*".

Peter wasn't the only one to bear witness that a restoration would occur, John the Beloved, while exiled to the Isle of Patmos, had a marvelous vision of things to come and he records it thusly: *"And I saw another angel fly in the midst of Heaven, having the everlasting gospel to preach unto them that dwell on the earth, and to every nation, and kindred, and tongue, and people, saying with a loud voice, fear God, and give glory to him ; for the hour of his judgment is come: And worship him that created heaven and earth and the sea, and the fountains of waters"* (Revelations 14: 6-7).

John the Beloved exiled to the Isle of Patmos some sixty years after the death of Christ; while in exile, viewed many marvelous visions which for the most part were pertinent to future times, which we know today as the "Book of Revelations".

In this vision, just quoted, John saw an Angel flying in the midst of Heaven. The angel had the everlasting gospel and was taking it to the earth *for every nation, kindred, tongue and people.*

The question that is begging to be asked is, why was an Angel bringing the everlasting gospel to earth if, as the Catholics maintain, the gospel was on the earth through their organization since Peter?

The answer is obvious and here again bears mute testimony to the actual occurrence of the Great Apostasy. The true gospel of Jesus Christ wasn't here . . . . it had to be restored and John witnessed the restoration taking place centuries before it actually happened.

This then is the crux of the message the "Church of Jesus Christ of Latter Day Saints" brings to the world today. The true gospel is restored with all the rights, authorities, and keys pertaining to the dispensation of the Fullness of Times; with authority to dispense the principles of salvation to the men and women of the world who sincerely believe that God can speak from Heaven, and that He has done so and will continue to do so.

On September 21, 1823 the Prophet Joseph Smith received his second Heavenly visitation in the form of an Angel who introduced himself as, "Moroni". He told the Prophet of an ancient record that lay buried not far from his home. The prophet was told that this record was a history of Gods dealings with the early inhabitants of the American Continent. The Angel said that the fullness of the everlasting gospel was contained in the record as delivered to the ancient inhabitants of this, the North American Continent, by the Savior.

This record was later brought forth by the Prophet Joseph Smith as the "Book of Mormon". In addition to being a record of the ancient inhabitants of this the American Continent, this marvelous book is, more specifically, a second witness of the divinity of the Savior.

While engaged in the work of translating the Book of Mormon, the Prophet Joseph Smith and an assistant and friend, by the name of Oliver Cowdery, came upon a passage of scripture concerning baptism for the remission of sins. Realizing that the authority to perform this ordinance had been taken from the earth and that this ordinance was necessary for salvation, the Prophet and his companion decided to make this matter the subject of prayer.

In accordance with this decision they retired to the woods to pray, and while they were employed in petitioning the Lord for knowledge concerning baptism, the Heavens were opened and a Heavenly Messenger, in a cloud of light, appeared to them and laying his hands upon their heads as they knelt he declared; *"Upon you my fellow servants, in the name of Messiah, I confer the Priesthood of Aaron, which holds the keys of the ministering of angels, and of the gospel of repentance, and of baptism by immersion for the remission of sins; and this shall never be taken again from the earth until the sons of Levi do offer again an offering unto the Lord in righteousness"* (Doctrine and Covenants 13).

The messenger said that his name was John, the same that is called John the Baptist in the New Testament, and that he acted under the direction of Peter, James and John who held the keys of the Melchizedek Priesthood. A Priesthood that would eventually be conferred on the Prophet.

Who better had the right to restore the Aaronic Priesthood to the earth than John the Baptist. The very same who baptized Christ. That he held this authority their can be no doubt. The Lord Jesus Christ recognized this to be the case when He presented Himself to John to be baptized, in the river Jordan, as recorded in Matt. 3: 13-17.

John declared to the Prophet Joseph Smith, that the priesthood he conferred, had not the power of laying on of hands for the Gift of The Holy Ghost, for this power is contained in the Melchizedek Priesthood.

In this marvelous manner the Prophet's prayer was answered and he not only learned about the ordinance of baptism, but was given the authority, the Aaronic Priesthood, to baptize.

He and his companion Oliver Cowdery stepped down into the Susquehanna river and baptized each other by complete immersion, for so they were directed by the messenger.

The Melchizedek Priesthood was restored to the earth through the Prophet Joseph Smith by Peter, James and John some six months after the appearance of John the Baptist.

Here again who was better qualified to restore the Melchizedek Priesthood than Peter, James and John who had been ordained Apostles by the Lord Jesus Christ and appointed as leaders of His Church established in the meridian of time.

With the restoration of this "greater" priesthood the Prophet Joseph Smith held the authority necessary to establish and develop the Church Of Jesus Christ in the earth.

The Church of Jesus Christ of Latter Day Saints was formally organized, in this the Dispensation of the Fullness of Times, on 6 April 1830, during the period of time of the feet of the great image that Daniel saw. The organization took place in Fayette, Seneca County, New York, pursuant to the laws of New York State, in the home of Peter Whitmer Sr. (The Restored Church, by William Edwin Barrett, pages 70-71).

The Church of Jesus Christ of Latter Day Saints, as organized today, is identical to the church the Lord set up, during His mortal ministry, in the meridian of time.

The Book of Mormon

The "Book of Mormon" is a major contributing factor to the doctrine espoused by the Church of Jesus Christ of Latter Day Saints. The book receives its name from the abridging author "Mormon".

The book of Mormon like the bible is comprised of many writings or books, each book being authored by a different writer or prophet. Mormon, an ancient Prophet, is attributed with the work of abridging the book in its entirety and for this reason the book or the compilation of writings bear his name. Hence the nickname "Mormon" is applied to The Church of Jesus Christ of Latter Day Saints, because of the Book of Mormon, which is a standard work of the Church.

Specifically the Book of Mormon, purports to be a record of Gods dealings with the ancient civilizations of the American Continent, just as the King James version of the Holy Bible purports to be a record of Gods dealings with ancient Israel and the Jews. The Book of Mormon is not the "bible" of the Latter Day Saints, but it is a scriptorial record of doctrine just as is the King James version of the Holy Bible, both of which are considered to be canon of scripture for the Church.

The Book of Mormon is a companion witness with the Bible to the reality and divinity of the Lord Jesus Christ. This marvelous record was delivered to Joseph Smith, 22 Sept 1827, in the form of gold plates by a Heavenly messenger who introduced himself as Moroni. Moroni is the author of the last book in the Book of Mormon and is also the son of Mormon, the prophet who abridged the book.

Joseph Smith translated the golden plates into what is known today as the "Book of Mormon". This work of translation took the Prophet Joseph Smith, approximately six months to accomplish. A rather remarkable achievement for an unlearned man raised on the American frontier.

He translated, the hieroglyphics in the plates of gold, using a device given to him, with the plates, called a Urim and Thummin or translator (see note 2 at the end of this chapter).

The details of the coming forth of this book are contained in the first pages of the book itself, with certifications of eleven men who actually saw and held the plates. Three of these eleven witnesses were shown the plates by an angel of the Lord as evidence of the divine nature of the record contained in the plates. As it is written, *"In the mouth of two or three witnesses shall every word be established"* (Matt 18:16, or 2 Corinthians 13:1).

The Book of Mormon commences with an account of a vision given to a man by the name of Lehi who lived in Jerusalem about 600 B C. In the vision Lehi was instructed by the Lord to flee Jerusalem with his family as the people of Jerusalem planned to kill him because he had prophesied against their wickedness.

Lehi and his family escaped into the wilderness and following the directions they were given, traveled to the ocean where they built boats and sailed under the guidance of the Lord to a promised land. Their journey carried them to the land known today as South America. Here the little group divided into two groups. One group called themselves the Nephites after Lehi's younger son Nephi who was a righteous man and a Prophet. The other group called themselves the Lamanites after Lehi's two older sons Leman and Lemual, who were contentious and rebellious both against their Father and the commandments of the Lord.

In time great nations came from these two family lines and spread through out the width and breadth of the land, both North and South America.

The Nephite people were industrious and artificers of all manner of metals and built cities wherever they settled. These people for the most part are identified as those who worshipped the Lord God. The Lamanites on the other hand were nomadic, lived off the land without cultivation and did not worship the Lord or strive to keep His commandments.

Because of the traditions of their Fathers these two nations were continually warring with each other. The Nephite nation would prosper when they were humble and worshipped the Lord. However, when they grew proud and ceased to hearken unto the Lord and turned their hearts from Him, then the Lamanites would have power over them, bringing them down to the depths of humility through conflict and persecution.

A high light of the histories of these people is contained in Third Nephi of the Book of Mormon, which describes the visit of the Lord to the American Continent after His crucifixion and resurrection.

The Bible makes reference to this great event in John 10:16, where we read a statement by the resurrected Lord; *"And other sheep I have which are not of this fold, them also I must bring, and they shall hear my voice; and there shall be one fold and one shepherd"*.

Here the Lord clearly indicated that He had other sheep or followers than those of the Jews to whom He was speaking at the time in Jerusalem and in Judea where He had labored throughout His ministry.

He further indicated that these other sheep would hear His voice. Now the disciples to whom Jesus was speaking supposed that He had reference to the Gentiles in and around Jerusalem when He said *"other sheep I have"*, but it must be remembered that the gospel was ultimately taken to the Gentiles by Peter and the Apostles and that they (the Gentiles) at no time saw or heard the Lords voice after His resurrection.

The Lord's ministry on earth prior to His crucifixion was to the Jews, to the lost sheep of the house of Israel and His instructions to the Apostles during this time were, *"Go not to the Gentiles but go rather to the lost sheep* (the rebellious Jews) *of the house of Israel"* (Matt 10:5-6).

When the Lord appeared to the Nephite people shortly after His resurrection, He had this to say to them, *"And verily I say unto you, that ye are they of whom I said: Other sheep I have which are not of this fold; them also I must bring, and they shall hear my voice, and there shall be one fold, and one shepherd: And they understood me not,* (speaking of his disciples in Jerusalem) *for they supposed it had been the Gentiles; for they understood not that the Gentiles should be converted through their preaching. And they understood me not that I said they shall hear my voice; and they understood me not that the Gentiles should not at any time hear my voice . . . . that I should not manifest myself unto them save it were by the Holy Ghost. But behold ye have both heard my voice, and seen me; and ye are my sheep, and ye are numbered among those whom the Father hath given me"* (Book of Mormon, 3 Nephi 15: 21-24).

During His visit to the Nephites and the Lamanites the Lord established His Church among the people and ordained Apostles and Prophets to govern the Church and administer in temporal and spiritual affairs.

For two hundred years after the Lords visit, the Nephites and Lamanites lived in peace and prospered. In fact so happy did these people become that the following was said of them, *". . . . and surely there could not be a happier people among all the people who had been created by the hand of God"* (Book of Mormon 4 Nephi 1: 16).

Eventually, inequality crept into their happy society, rift and division, occurred and wars began to prevail. Approximately four hundred years after the visitation of the Lord, the Lamanites in a series of battles virtually annihilated the Nephites except for a righteous prophet-general named Moroni.

Moroni buried the plates of gold, containing the more precious records of these people, in the ground according to the instructions of the Lord. The same Moroni as a resurrected being, delivered these records to the Prophet Joseph Smith at the time of the restoration of the gospel in 1827.

The period of time covered in the Book of Mormon is a little more than one thousand years, commencing 600 BC and ending 421 AD.

The coming forth of the Book of Mormon was seen by an ancient Prophet of the Lord, as recorded in the bible, Ezekiel 37 :15-21. The Lord speaking to Ezekiel said, *"Moreover thou son of man, take thee one stick, and write upon it for Judah, and for the children of Israel, his companions; then take another stick, and write upon it, for Joseph, the stick of Ephraim, and all the house of Israel his companions; and join them one to another into one stick; and they shall become one in thy hand"*. A stick in the days of Ezekiel was a scroll or record. The stick of Judah therefore is a record of the tribe of Judah and his companions or more specifically . . . . the Jews. The record of the Jews as we have it today is the bible. The Latter Day Saints maintain that the stick of Ephraim is the Book of Mormon, which is a record of Gods dealings with the descendants of Joseph, he who was sold into slavery by his brothers.

To more fully appreciate this view point concerning the stick of Ephraim, it is important to understand the relationship of Judah and Joseph and the house of Israel and the part they would play in the divine plan of the Lord.

Chapter 49 in the book of Genesis as contained in the Holy Bible, describes the blessing given by Jacob to his twelve sons.

The name "Israel", was conferred upon Jacob by the Lord as recorded in Genesis 32:28, *"And He said, thy name shall be called no more Jacob but Israel; for as a prince hast thou power with God and with men and hast prevailed".*

The twelve sons of Israel through generations of descendants became great tribes or nations. For example Judah, one of the sons of Israel, is the progenitor of the Jews. The people of the Book of Mormon are descendants of Joseph through his sons Ephraim and Manasseh.

Joseph, as a boy, was sold into slavery by his brothers who rent his coat, dipped it in sheep's blood and presented it to their Father Israel, as evidence that Joseph had been killed by a wild beast. No doubt his brothers felt considerable regret at their deed because of the great anguish suffered by their Father at the supposed loss of his youngest son (see Genesis 37: 31-35).

One may ask, ... why would Joseph's brothers perpetrate such an unrighteous deed against their younger brother? A review of the bible account indicates the reason to be the age old wickedness of jealousy and envy. *"Now Israel loved Joseph more than all his children, because he was the son of his old age; and he made him a coat of many colors. And when his brethren saw that their Father loved him more than all his brethren, they hated him and could not speak peaceably unto him. And Joseph dreamed a dream, and he told it to his brethren or brothers; and they hated him yet the more. And he said unto them, hear, I pray you, this dream which I have dreamed: For behold, we were binding sheaves in the field, and lo, my sheaf arose and also stood upright; and behold, your sheaves stood round about, and made obeisance to my sheaf. And his brethren said to him, shalt thou indeed reign over us? Or shalt thou indeed have dominion over us? And they hated him yet the more for his dream, and for his words. And he dreamed yet another dream, and told it his brethren, and said, behold, I have dreamed a dream more; and behold the sun and the moon and the eleven stars made obeisance to me. And he told it his Father, and his brethren; and his Father rebuked him, and said unto him, what is this dream that thou hast dreamed? Shall I and thy Mother and thy brethren indeed come to bow down ourselves to thee to the earth? And his brethren envied him; but his Father observed the saying" (Genesis 37: 3-11).*

Joseph's dreams, while they caused him considerable grief within his own family were symbolic of what eventually came to pass. Joseph was sold into Egypt, into slavery, but through the blessings of the Lord gained a pre-immense second only to the Pharaoh himself. Due to a severe famine in the land Israel and his family were driven to Egypt for sustenance, where they in very deed did obeisance to Joseph, as the great prime minister of Egypt, not realizing he was of their family, until he revealed himself to them.

And because of these circumstances, lightly touched upon here, it came to pass that the Israelites flourished in Egypt and became the great Nations that Moses eventually led out of that land . . . . but, of course, that is another story.

However! in consideration of his dream and subsequent challenges and blessings in Egypt, it is clear that Joseph was very faithful and therefore highly favored by the Lord.

A review of the blessings pronounced upon Joseph by his Patriarch Father, is further evidence of his high standing among the sons of Israel and indeed ultimately all the tribes of Israel.

Joseph's blessings are greater than his brothers received even greater than those of Judah through whose loins the Messiah would come. *"Joseph is a fruitful bough, even a fruitful bough by a well, whose branches run over the wall: The archers have sorely grieved him, and shot at him, and hated him: but his bow abode in strength, and the arms of his hands were made strong by the hands of the mighty God of Jacob: (from thence is the shepherd, the stone of Israel). Even by the God of thy Father, who shall help thee; and by the Almighty, who shall bless thee with blessings of Heaven above, blessings of the deep that lieth under, blessings of the breasts, and of the womb: The blessings of thy Father have prevailed above the blessings of my progenitors unto the utmost bound of the everlasting hills: They shall be on the head of Joseph and on the crown of the head of him that was separate from his brethren"* (Genesis 49: 22-26).

Joseph's blessings are numerous as well might be expected for the most righteous of the sons of Israel.

In the blessing he received from his Father, Joseph is described as a fruitful bough implying that he would have a large posterity. He was told that his "branches", or descendants would run over the "wall". The wall being a barrier such as continents and large bodies of water, but his descendants would conquer these obstacles and go beyond them. The archers that sorely grieved him were his brothers who hated him, and sold him into slavery. Joseph was told that his blessings prevailed above the blessings of his progenitors unto the utmost bounds of the everlasting hills.

Here Joseph was told that he was to enjoy all the blessing of his progenitors, and more . . . . his *"branches"*, or posterity were to run over the wall or barrier, to a place described as the *"everlasting hills"*.

The land fitting that description and one that is located in the position of *"the utmost bounds"* from the old world, and one of *"everlasting hills"*, is none other than the Americas. How could they be more aptly described than a land of *"everlasting hill"*. Hills that start in the Aleutian Islands, come down through Alaska, through North America as the "Rockies", and "Sierras", through Central America down to the tip of South America as the Andes; a continuous mountain chain. A topography map depicts this chain of mountains as a "reptile", stretched from the top of North America to the bottom most point of South America. Truly a land of *"everlasting hills"*.

And it was to this land that the descendants of Joseph came.

The Book of Mormon describes the Nephites and Lamanites as being descendants of Ephraim and Manasseh, the sons of Joseph of Egypt.

And so the "Mormons", bear witness to the world that the "stick" of Ephraim written for Joseph and his companions has come forth as the Book of Mormon.

The Book of Mormon is a true record of Gods dealings with the ancient civilizations of North and South America.

Even in our generation ruins have been unearthed in Central America that testify to the existence of such an ancient civilization.

The Book of Mormon is new scripture and supports every facet of the Gospel as set forth in the Holy Bible. Indeed, the Book of Mormon is a purer scriptural record than the bible having been translated once, and then by a Prophet of God.

The Book of Mormon makes a promise to all readers, *"And when ye shall receive these things, I would exhort you that ye would ask God, the Eternal Father, in the name of Christ, if these things are not true; and if ye shall ask with a sincere heart, with real intent, having faith in Christ, He will manifest the truth of it unto you, by the power of the Holy Ghost"* (Book of Mormon, Moroni 10:4)

Put it to the test dear reader. You have nothing to lose and everything to gain.

NOTE 2

Just a brief word about this special device. This device the "Urim and Thummin" is mentioned no less than eight times in the old and new testament. The name is a Hebrew term that means, "light and perfections". It is an instrument prepared by God to assist man in obtaining revelations from the Lord, and in interpreting languages, and its use is the prerogative of a Seer. A Seer is also a Prophet, and is greater than a Prophet. A Prophet, however, is not always a Seer. (see Bible dictionary page 771).

First Principles and Ordinances of the Gospel

This chapter is devoted to a consideration of basic beliefs taught by the Church of Jesus Christ of Latter Day Saints relative to the Gospel of Jesus Christ. This chapter will be sub-divided into three topics and four sub-topics. The fall, the atonement, and the first principles and ordinances of the gospel. The sub-topics are: Faith, repentance, baptism, and the gift of the Holy Ghost.

The Fall

The phrase "The Fall", has reference to an event that the first man of the race and his spouse, Eve experienced and is a controversial issue through out Christendom.

Some Christian Sects maintain that the fall of Adam and Eve and subsequent expulsion from the Garden of Eden was due to a demonstration of moral weakness that has propagated misery and problems on the entire human race.

Many Christian Sects prefer to look upon the story of "the fall", as a myth having its foundation in the oft repeated and embellished word of mouth stories of ancient and barbaric societies of the past.

These concepts are all erroneous and exist through the inability, or lack of spiritual guidance, or unwillingness of many theologians to understand, or to trust the scriptures.

The Church of Jesus Christ of Latter Day Saints (the Church) teaches that Adam was not a moral degenerate but was a noble man chosen of God to stand at the head of the entire human family as the Grand Patriarch. The Church further teaches that, "the fall" was necessary to provide the way for billions of the spirit offspring of God to come to earth, acquire mortal bodies and to be added upon through the experiences of a mortal life. The Latter Day Saints advocate that "the fall" did not happen by mistake but was carefully planned and orchestrated by our Heavenly Father.

Our God is a very detailed God. Just read of His dealings with mankind and you will see that He leaves nothing to chance that pertains to His ordinances and gospel as it relates to the salvation of His offspring. His guidance, instruction, and commandments, on how to live our lives so that we can qualify to come back into His presence occupies the books we know as the Old and New Testament, the Book of Mormon and others (see chapter 7. Scriptures). In fact so thorough are the Lords preparation for the salvation for man that the only thing left to chance is mans use of his free agency. And God has been scrupulous in avoiding any infringement into mans agency.

So what are the chances that He was casual about how to introduce His progeny, many billions of them, into the new world He had created just for them. I can't imagine a being as powerful and as intelligent, as our God, leaving anything to chance.

His plans and preparations for such a momentous event as the introduction of mortal life on to this brand new planet would be, meticulous by His standards and miraculous by our standards.

But to continue. All things were created spiritually before they were created naturally upon this earth. In Genesis, we read, *"These are the generations of the heavens and of the earth when they were created, in the day that the Lord God made the earth and the heavens:*

And every plant of the field <u>before</u> it was in the earth, and every herb of the field <u>before</u> it grew" (Genesis 2:4-5).

Through modern day revelation the spiritual creation of all things is more pointedly described. *"And every plant of the field before it grew. For I, the Lord God, created all things of which I have spoken, <u>spiritually,</u> before they were naturally upon the face of the earth. For I, the Lord God, had not caused it to rain upon the face of the earth and I, the Lord God, had created all the children of men: and not yet a man to till the ground; for in heaven created I them, and there was not flesh upon the earth, neither in the water, neither in the air"* (Pearl of Great Price, Moses 3:5-6)

The scriptures clearly indicate that man and indeed all life, had a spiritual beginning and development prior to becoming a mortal resident of the earth. However, the existence of man prior to earth life, is the basis of the great plan of salvation, a fascinating discussion contained in the last chapter of this book and will not be enlarged upon here.

The scriptures leave us somewhat in the dark concerning the temporal creation of the earth, plant and animal life and of man. The bible describes the creation work of seven days, or seven periods of time, but not in detail.

Through modern revelation, we have learned that these details will not always remain a secret; *"Yea verily I say unto you, in that day when the Lord shall come, he shall reveal all things—Things which have passed, and hidden things which no man knew, things of the earth by which it was made, and the purpose and the end thereof"* (Doctrine & Covenants 101:32-33).

While the precise details of Adams physical creation remain a mystery to us, we are left with little doubt that man was created in the image of God and clearly established as having dominion over the earth. We read, *"And God said let us make man in our image, after our likeness; and let them have dominion over the fish of the sea . . . . etc. So God created man in his own image, in the image of God created he him; male and female created he them"* (Genesis 1:26-27).

Please note that Adam was given dominion over the earth and all life upon it.

People I have met, commenting on this scripture, have maintained in discussions with me, *"that man is not created in the physical image of God but has only been endowed with a divine capacity for love"*. This interpretation of the scriptures contained in Genesis 1:26-27, is flagrant conjecture. A rereading of this scripture reveals no mention of love, either stated or implied, and the language is such as to make it difficult, if not completely imaginative, to construe the meaning of this scripture to be anything other than a clear statement, that man was created after the form and fashion of God. We look like God!

Why wouldn't we look like Him? After all we are His "offspring".

So man, Adam and Eve, were created and placed in the Garden of Eden, *"to dress it and keep it"*.

The next injunction given to man was interesting and reveals that man's original physical condition as it relates to death, was far different from that which we now experience.

"And the Lord commanded the man saying, of every tree of the garden thou mayest freely eat: but of the tree of the knowledge of good and evil, thou shalt not eat of it: for in the day that thou eatest thereof thou shalt surely die". (Genesis 2:16-17).

The mandate of the Lord was clear. Adam and Eve were not to partake of the food or fruit designated as forbidden or they would die. This is a very interesting statement by the Lord and clearly indicates that the condition of death was not, at that time, applicable to Adam and Eve and wouldn't be unless they ate some of the fruit of that tree.

Our first parents were also given another commandment, wherein they were directed by God to *"Be fruitful, and multiply and replenish the earth and subdue it"*. These commandments must have caused some confusion to Adam and Eve. They knew they were immortal, and not subject to the condition of death and would continue to be so, unless they ate some of that forbidden fruit. Heavenly Father had plainly told them that. They had also been commanded to multiply and replenish the earth, something they could scarcely accomplish in their innocent condition.

How do we know they were so innocent as to not be tempted by the lusts of the flesh experienced by mortal man. Where were their carnal inclinations so prevalent in mortality? The answer is . . . . they weren't mortal, they were immortal, and they had no knowledge of mortality, or of the flesh . . . . they were as innocent as babes in matters of the flesh. To illustrate how very innocent our first parents were in their immortal condition, the biblical record states, *"And they were both naked the man and his wife and were not ashamed"* (Genesis 2:25).

In addition they were to subdue the earth which, from their view point in the Garden of Eden, could scarcely require subduing being a land of plenty, on every hand.

In short it appears that Adam and Eve were trapped in a web of conflicting commandments. On the one hand, they were subject to a commandment that to obey would cause them to remain innocent and therefore; unproductive and that is the commandment to abstain from the forbidden fruit. On the other hand they were given a commandment to multiply and replenish the earth, which they could comply with only if they gained knowledge, and to do that they would have to partake of the forbidden fruit, ... and in so doing their eyes would be opened and they would have knowledge, or gain wisdom.

Now enters a third party into the dilemma, Lucifer. Lucifer using the guise of a serpent, recognized an opportunity to put man in opposition to God, through use of his agency and Lucifer moved to capitalize on the situation by tempting Eve to partake of the forbidden fruit.

His arguments as to why such transgression was desirable, was more than Eve could bear in her guileless frame of mind. Satan argued that if she would partake of the fruit she would become as God, in knowing good from evil (Genesis 3:5), she would become wise. Who could resist the temptation to become like God, who in all probability was an object of great love and admiration to Eve, just as any tender innocent daughter loves a kindly Father. Eve succumbed to temptation and partook of the fruit.

Eve's transgression now put Adam in a dilemma. His Father had specifically forbade him to partake of the forbidden fruit, but He had also commanded him to *"cleave unto his wife and they shall be one flesh"* (Genesis 2: 23-24).

Adam knew that Eve would be separated from him because of her transgression . . . . what was he to do? Adam partook of the fruit in order to remain with Eve, and to fulfill a higher law to multiply and replenish the earth.

In contemplating Adam's transgression we can conclude that the extent of his disobedience was no more than the breaking of a law of health. Adam certainly could not be condemned for eventually using his powers of procreation to reproduce his kind since he was under the divine mandate *"to multiply and replenish the earth"*.

Shame on any man who thinks the God given power of procreation is sinful and degenerate. Mans moral degeneracy arises from perversion of the powers of procreation and not because of anything Adam and Eve did.

God had told Adam and Eve that in the day they partook of the forbidden fruit they would surely die. But the biblical account reveals that Adam and Eve went on to live hundreds of years. Why wasn't the divine mandate that if they partook of the forbidden fruit . . . . *in that day they would surly die* . . . . why didn't they die?

Adam and Eve did die on that day. When they partook of the fruit a change came over their bodies and they became mortal and as such they became subject to death. They began to age and grow old.

Then too, as a result of their transgression they were cast out of the Garden of Eden and out of the presence of God, which is a spiritual death. So yes indeed, death did come upon our first parents on the day they partook of the forbidden fruit.

This event of being ostracized forever from the presence of God, because of disobedience, and subject to the temptations of Satan is known as *"the fall"*.

Having been cast out of the luxurious Garden of Eden and the presence of God, Adam found himself in a world that indeed needed subduing. And he, must have, realized that truly by the sweat of his brow would he subdue the thorn, thistle and noxious weed and provide a livelihood for himself and his family.

Had Adam failed to break a lesser law to fill a greater one, he would have been separated from Eve and Gods plan for the progression of His spirit children would have been frustrated. But our God knew Adam very well, and gallant Adam accepted temporal trials and tribulations upon himself in order to obey a higher law, that of multiplying and replenishing the earth.

In the transgression, Eve was beguiled and was cursed with pain and sorrow in child bearing. Adam transgressed with the complete realization he was breaking a commandment and for this the earth was cursed, for his sake, *"in sorrow shalt thou eat of it all the days of thy life"* (Genesis 3 :17-19).

The serpent, for permitting Satan to use him, was cursed that it would crawl on its belly and eat dust.

Lucifer in his desire to sabotage the Lord's plan to provide a mortal experience for His countless numbers of spirit children by tempting Eve, had unwittingly become a tool in the Lord's hand to accomplish the very thing he, Lucifer, had thought to destroy.

Satan's act of temptation provided Adam and Eve the opportunity to use their free agency, which is exactly what God wanted to happen.

In considering the fall of Adam in retrospect, we might conclude that Adam's action actually was a progressive step; for when God discovered that Adam and Eve had partaken of the forbidden fruit, He commented, *"Behold, the man has become as one of us to know good and evil and now lest he put forth his hand and take also of the tree of life and eat and live forever: therefore the Lord God sent him forth from the Garden of Eden to till the ground from whence he was taken"* (Genesis 3: 22-23).

As a result of his transgression Adam actually acquired several God like attributes. The power of procreation and the knowledge of good and evil, he became wise. The fall was an improvement, and an unmitigated advancement for the circumstances of man and not a detriment.

Apparently there was another tree in the Garden that contained a fruit that had the power to infuse eternal life. The Lord was concerned that the man Adam and his wife Eve might partake of this tree. So He drove them from the Garden and set up a Cherubim with a flaming sword to keep them away (Genesis 3: 22-24).

The reason for this rather drastic action was to stop man from partaking of the tree of life and living forever in his fallen state or forever exiled from the presence of God, having no space for repentance or a time of preparation to come back into the presence of God.

Had Adam partaken of the tree of life, the great plan of salvation would have been thwarted and man consigned forever to live in a fallen state, never having the opportunity to go back into the presence of God, and always subject to the buffeting of Satan.

So, man deliberately left the presence of God with the realization that in so doing he could obtain greater degrees of light and knowledge and ultimately become as God.

The Latter Day Saints maintain that Adam's action was a noble and valiant step requiring great courage and greater faith. Nevertheless, man's position relative to salvation was extremely tenuous because he had of his own free will left the presence of God and had no way to get back except there was a reconciliation between man and Heavenly Father.

Reconciliation had to be made by someone of considerable stature in the eyes of God the Father in terms of worthiness, love and courage. The only one worthy to reconcile fallen man to God the Father was a man who Himself was a God and who had a vested interest of love in the fallen, in this case their older Brother; a man who was sinless and not subject to Satan, who was willing, to make a sacrifice of His mortal life. The only mortal who qualified was Jesus Christ. And He accomplished this task of reconciliation and in so doing became the savior of the world.

And now let us behold a marvelous truth. God knew and prepared all things pertinent to the fall of Adam to happen exactly as they did. He knew that a Redeemer would be necessary to bridge the broken law and effect an Atonement to reconcile fallen man to God.

For this reason He had prepared a Redeemer before this world was created, *"Forasmuch as ye know that ye were not redeemed with corruptible things, as silver and gold, but with the precious blood of Christ as of a lamb without blemish and with out spot who verily was foreordained before the foundation of the world, but was manifest in these last times for you"* (1 Peter 1: 18-20).

And, also in Paul's first discourse to the Corinthians, *"But now is Christ risen from the dead and become the first fruits of them that slept. For since by man came death, by man came also the resurrection of the dead. For as in Adam all die, even so in Christ shall all be made alive"* (1 Corinthians 15:20-22).

Our Heavenly Father leaves nothing to chance. His planning and preparation is perfect. The fall that introduced all of us into mortality, also ostracized us from the presence of God, but a plan had been prepared from the beginning of the world . . . . before the Garden of Eden, to bring us back into the presence of God, and to nullify the effect of the fall based on certain conditions. And that is the subject of the next topic, the atonement.

The Atonement

It would be an unjust God indeed, that would permit all the descendants of Adam and Eve to suffer eternally from their, Adam and Eve's, individual act of transgression. For this reason, a redeemer was chosen to make the supreme sacrifice and thereby satisfy the law of justice. Essentially the law of justice decrees that since Adam and Eve, had of their own free will, transgressed the commandment of God and in effect deliberately left Gods presence, they and those who they represented, their descendants, could never come back into the presence of God.

However, the atonement of Jesus paid the price of this transgression, as Jesus took upon Himself the sins of all mankind, and in doing so satisfied the demands of justice. His unselfish sacrifice, and that by a man without sin, gave all of mankind access to the law of mercy. This law permits fallen man, access to the presence of God and His kingdom upon acceptance of Jesus as the Redeemer and Savior. And no mortal can accept Jesus unless they do so in the way He has prescribed. Which is only fair. Jesus paid the price, He ransomed us . . . . He has the right to tell us what is acceptable to Him. We have the right to listen, learn and obey or ignore Him. Both options have consequences, some good some not so good.

This great atoning sacrifice by Jesus accomplished in the meridian of time, was commemorated before the fact by ancient Israel, in the killing of a lamb without spot or blemish, in remembrance of the Lords sacrifice. And in this manner, did the faithful of ancient days demonstrate and exercise faith in the Lord.

The Saints of times subsequent to the Lord's crucifixion partook of the bread and wine, the sacrament, in remembrance of His flesh and blood which He gave for the sins and transgressions of man.

Biblical history plainly teaches that Nations of people blessed with Prophets of God as spiritual leaders have understood the necessity of an atonement or redemption and have engaged in divinely prescribed ritual to pay homage to the Redeemer, who reconciled fallen man to God.

Only He who was without spot or blemish could fulfill this mission. He alone is the one man over whom Satan could exercise no dominion, because He was sinless.

Then too as a result of His miraculous birth, being born of mortal woman, and sired by the immortal God, He became part mortal and part God.

From His Mother He inherited the capacity to die, and from His divine Father He inherited the capacity to have power over life and death. He exclaimed, *"Therefore doth my Father love me, because I lay down my life that I might take it again. No man taketh it from me, but I lay it down of myself. I have power to lay it down and I have power to take it again. This commandment have I received of my Father"* (John 10 : 17–18).

The atonement had to be a free will offering. Nothing short of that could be acceptable. Jesus accepted that challenge on behalf of all mankind both born and unborn, both the living and the dead.

He approached the hour of His sacrifice in considerable anxiety and prayed to His Father that this cup might pass from Him. But His Father sent Him strength to endure not to withdraw.

Much of the atonement must have been accomplished in the Garden of Gethsemane where Jesus assumed all of the sins of mankind. These sins were so grievous as to cause a mighty God to shrink, tremble, and bleed from every pore of His mortal body. But He bore the load though spiritually racked, until He must have felt as though He would tear asunder. Our limited understandings cannot comprehend, nor has it been revealed the manner in which the sins of all of mankind were assumed by Jesus. By what phenomena the sins of past, present and future generations gravitated and culminated at one point in time upon one individual is a mystery not given to us. Suffice us to know that He paid the price and opened the way of redemption for all mankind.

The atonement basically provides two marvelous blessings:

1. <u>The resurrection.</u> Paul in preaching to the Corinthians declared, *"for the trumpet shall sound, and the dead shall be raised incorruptible* (beautiful people), *and we shall be changed. For this corruption must put on incorruption, and this mortal must put on immortality"* (1 Corinthians 15 : 52-53).

Not only will we live again but we will all be beautiful people. The resurrection is a free gift to every mortal. We don't have to do a single solitary thing to receive the gift of the resurrection.

However the resurrection has nothing to do with our status before God nor our eventual judgment. As John also declared, *"Marvel not at this: for the hour is coming, in the which all that are in the graves shall hear his voice and shall come forth; they that have done good unto the resurrection of life and they that have done evil, unto the resurrection of damnation"* (John 5: 28-29).

Apparently the resurrection does not, and was never intended to justify a sinner; and since the resurrection is the gate into immortality the resurrection will more fully condemn a sinner. Based on what John has said the resurrection locks each of us into the degree of worthiness we have earned by the life we lived in mortality.

2. <u>The opportunity for salvation.</u> Salvation is defined, as the ability that is earned through personal effort, to qualify to come back into the presence of God.

Unlike the resurrection the judgments of the Lord are profoundly influenced by works done in the flesh. Salvation is <u>not a free gift</u> but is wholly dependant on our behavior as a mortal. Salvation is also a completely individual accomplishment, through effort and obedience to the laws of the Gospel. One might ask, "If salvation is obtained through works on the part of each individual soul, of what value was the atonement of Christ, except, of course, for the resurrection"?

To answer this let us refer to the scripture's. Paul speaking of Christ to the Hebrews declared, *"Though he were a Son, yet learned He obedience by the things which he suffered; and being made perfect, he became the author of eternal salvation unto all them that obey him"* (Hebrews 5:9). Note that Paul speaks of salvation and not resurrection.

Jesus then is the author, or the definer, of eternal salvation unto only those who obey Him. And what does it mean, to obey? It means to submit our wills to the will of the Lord and that is precisely what is required.

Now for a free agent to, freely, submit his will to the will of another, is sacrifice. Consequently, the true Church of Jesus Christ will always be associated with individual sacrifice. The sacrifice of forsaking our sins.

We have talked about obedience, but obedience to what? What is Jesus the author of? He is the author or definer of the Gospel. The gospel, basically, is a compilation of laws and rules of behavior, that God knows will qualify man to come back into His presence. Laws that will make man clean or worthy to endure the glorified presence of God and live in His society.

So part two of the atonement gives man the chance to qualify to be redeemed from the fall, provided he can make the sacrifice necessary to deny Satan's temptations of multiple lusts of the flesh, and instead develop habits based on higher laws that qualify for the Kingdom of God.

Part two is a challenge for the natural man, who may experience bursts of fervor to do what is right and then is confronted with . . . . *enduring to the end* which is the real challenge. How we develop the ability to persevere, is the next subject we want to consider.

First principles and ordinances of the gospel

In this section we will continue our discussion of the laws or principles of conduct as defined in the Gospel of Jesus Christ. First let us set the stage by considering a basic principle of the Gospel.

Through modern day revelation we have received the following enlightenment: *"There is a law irrevocably decreed before the foundations of this world upon which all blessings are predicated and when we obtain any blessing from God it is by obedience to the law upon which it is predicated"* (Doctrine & Covenants 130:20-21).

This doctrine sounds more like a law from the science of cause and effects than a governing tenet of a religious order. If we touch a hot stove with a bare finger, we are burned. If we live the laws of God, we reap the blessings attendant thereto. It's that simple. Paul said essentially the same thing to the Galatians, *"For whatsoever a man soweth, that shall he also reap"* (Gal 6:7).

One such law that we might consider is in the form of a commandment as expressed by the Savior, in Matthew, *"Be ye therefore perfect even as your Father which is in Heaven is Perfect"* (Matthew 5:48). This injunction was given by the Lord as a summary to the sermon on the mount and clearly implies that imperfect man can become perfect like God, through obedience to the laws He had just taught. That makes sense doesn't it? In order to live in the presence of God, one must become like Him. One must become qualified to abide in His society.

I have learned that virtually all Christian sects scoff at the idea that man has the potential to become like God. Why?

Is Christ being capricious, is He toying with us with that statement, is He asking us to strive for an impossible goal? That would be fraudulent. If we take Christ's admonition at face value, we must conclude that the potential of man is enormous.

Such scoffing has no biblical foundation, and when the truth is known it becomes apparent that man is a more noble creature than he is given credit for and does, in fact, contain in embryo the seeds of Godhood. This isn't strange doctrine. Man was created by God in His image, and the Lord taught us how to pray to Him and to address Him as *"Our Father which art in Heaven"*. What is more natural than to become like Him? In point of fact it is unnatural not to try and become like Him.

Paul the apostle made reference to the great potential of man when he explained to the Ephesians why the Lord established his Church on earth: *"For the perfecting of the Saints, for the work of the ministry, for the edifying of the body of Christ; till we all come in the unity of the faith and of the knowledge of the Son of God, unto a perfect man, unto the measure of the stature of the fullness of Christ"* Ephesians 4:12-13).

Is it not evident that any man who achieves the *"measure of the stature of the fullness of Christ"*, will be in very deed a God as Christ is? Again Paul bore witness to the great potential of man when he declared to the Romans, *"The spirit itself beareth witness with our spirit, that we are children of God, and if children then heirs: heirs of God, and joint heirs with Christ if so be that we suffer with him that we may be also glorified together"* (Romans 8: 16-17).

However Godhood is not obtained without a price. Paul declares that our divine inheritance cannot be realized unless we suffer with Christ that we may also be glorified with Him. He instructed the Romans: *"For not the hearers of the law are just before God, but the doers of the law shall be justified"* (Romans 2:13).

I submit that any man or woman is gravely mistaken, who think to earn divine acceptance by any way other than keeping God's commandments. As it is written, *"He that hath my commandments and keepeth them, he it is that loveth me; and he that loveth me shall be loved of my Father, and I will love him, and will manifest myself to him"* (John 14:21).

No child can please his parents except by doing the bidding of that parent.

Man cannot truly manifest love for God except by keeping His commandments.

Faith

Before anyone can keep the commandments of God, he must believe that God exists and that He will reward those who seek Him. *"But without faith it is impossible to please him; for he that cometh to God must believe that he is a rewarder of them that diligently seek him"* (Hebrews 11:6).

Faith is the first principle of the gospel. Faith and belief are frequently used in the biblical scriptures interchangeably to mean virtually the same thing. However, in more modern times the two words have taken on different meanings. The word belief, now implies a passive form of acknowledgement. James in writing to the Saints in all the Churches, illustrated this point when he said, *"Thou believest that there is one God; thou doest well: The devils, also believe and tremble. But wilt thou know, O vain man that faith without works is dead"* (James 2:19-20). To believe that God exists is no assurance of salvation. The devils know that He exists and that knowledge avails them nothing, but . . . . worry.

A man may believe that it is accounted to him as righteousness if he keeps the Sabbath day holy. But if he engages in sports activities, or other amusements on the Sabbath, instead, his belief is vain and is accounted to him as a condemnation rather than a blessing. However, when that same man, because of his belief attends church and worships God, and indeed keeps the Sabbath day holy, then he has demonstrated faith and it is accounted to him as righteousness.

As it applies to the laws of the gospel, belief plus action equals faith. The action part of faith is, of course, ... works! Which is the only way to live the laws of the gospel and the only way to demonstrate genuine love for the Lord.

Repentance

Through faith man will come to recognize the existence of God and will learn respect for His laws, and will develop a desire to be recognized by Him. This recognition will bring a feeling of a sense of unworthiness and a desire to be free of former transgressions. *"As it is written, there is none righteous, no, not one"* (Romans 3:10). And again, *"For there is not a just man upon the earth, that doeth good and sinneth not"* (Ecclesiastes 7:20).

All men have sinned and fallen short of the mark save only Jesus, who is the only perfect man to have walked this earth. This being true, man is doomed forever to be banished from the presence of God. Which statement would be literally true except for this principle of repentance.

Once a man has a conviction, and that through faith, that God lives, his natural desire to please God will motivate him to forsake sin. Repentance is therefore the second principle of the gospel.

True repentance embodies the following basic tenets:

1. To truly repent a man must first recognize that he has sinned.

2. He must have a sincere desire to be free of that sin and escape the stigma of unworthiness. *"No unclean thing can dwell in the presence of God, if so, then the Kingdom of God must also be filthy. But the Kingdom of God is not filthy and no unclean thing can enter there"* (Book of Mormon, 1 Nephi 10: 26 and 15: 33-34)

3. Through good works the sin must be overcome and never again practiced. If a wrong has been perpetrated against a fellow being, then restitution must be made if possible. Through prayer former sins must be enumerated and laid bare before God and forgiveness requested with the determination never again to enter into that sin. As we learn from the scriptures, *"If we confess our sins he is faithful and just to forgive us our sins, and to cleanse us from all unrighteousness. If we say that we have not sinned we make him a liar, and his word is not in us"* (1 John 1:9-10).

4. We must exercise the principle of forgiveness in our lives and truly forgive those who have trespassed against us. Our own repentance is hypocrisy if we do not forgive those who have sinned against us. The principle of repentance is the only avenue open to us sinners to evidence our determination to become clean and to make preparation for the next step. Which is the actual process of being washed clean.

Louis A. Kelsch

Baptism

The third principle of the Gospel is the ordinance of baptism. After we have learned that God lives and we have gained a desire to please Him and have repented of our sins; then we openly covenant with the Lord through baptism that such is the case and that we will keep His commandments. Baptism is the act by which we receive a remission or forgiveness, and a cleansing from our sins. Jesus submitted Himself to baptism at the hands of John the Baptist, *"To fulfill all righteousness"* (Matthew 3:13-15).

Now if Christ, who was perfect and had no sin, required baptism for the purpose of *"fulfilling righteousness",* how much more do we, who are sinners, require baptism? The injunction of the Lord is clear, *Except a man be born of the water and the spirit, he cannot enter into the Kingdom of God"* (John 3:5).

The mode of baptism is a controversial issue in modern Christianity. Some argue for complete immersion, and some for sprinkling, and others declare the willingness to accept any baptism in any church.

The Mormons believe and practice baptism by immersion. Jesus was baptized by John in the river Jordan (Mark 1:9). The Lord showed us the way. Even though He was without sin He submitted to baptism, as a mortal, *"For this life is the time for men to prepare to meet God",* (Book of Mormon, Alma 34:32)

The word "baptism", comes from the Greek word, "baptizo" and connotates dipping or immersion. Polybious a writer of history, who flourished during the second century, uses the following expressions, in describing a naval conflict between the Carthaginians and Roman fleets off the shores of Sicily, he says:

"If any were hard pressed by the enemy they withdrew safely back, on account of their fast sailing into the open sea: and then turning around

and falling on those of their pursers who were in advance, they gave some frequent blows and baptized many of their vessels" (Ready reference compilation on Baptism, pages 39-40)

The same writer refers to the passage of the Roman soldiers through the river Trebia, *"When the passage of the river Trebia came on, which had risen above its normal current on account of the rain which had fallen, the infantry with difficulty passed over being baptized up to the chest"*

It is apparent that the meaning of baptism in the meridian of time had no double meanings, and therefore, required no written clarification, as to what a baptism really is.

Baptism is an important commandment of the Lord. Christ submitted Himself to be baptized by John the Baptist declaring, *"For thus it becometh us to fulfill all righteousness"*(Matthew 3:15). Later on He charged His Apostles, *"Go ye into all the world and preach the gospel to every creature. He that believeth and is baptized shall be saved but he that believeth not shall be damned"* (Mark 16:15-16).

Many Christian churches maintain that little children need to be baptized to negate the sin of Adam in their behalf. However, in the scripture just quoted, the admonition of the Savior to His apostles bore the assumption that they to whom the gospel message was delivered would have the ability to reason and hence believe or disbelieve. Certainly no infant, however precocious, could be expected to exercise the mental powers of logic and reason on such weighty matters as personal salvation, and ultimately develop a belief system, either pro or con on the merits of baptism.

The Lord is just, and merciful, and does not expect the same behavior of an infant that He would expect of a mature adult. Religious sects that advocate infant baptism deny the atonement of

Christ and set at naught His great efficacious sacrifice to reconcile fallen man with God.

The following scripture from the Book of Mormon clearly defines the position of the Latter Day Saints relative to infant baptism. *"And he that saith that all little children need baptism denieth the mercies of Christ, and setteth at naught the atonement of him and the power of his redemption. For behold that all little children are alive in Christ, and also all they that are without law. For the power of redemption cometh on all them that have no law; wherefore he that is not condemned or he that is under no condemnation, cannot repent; and unto such baptism availed nothing"* (Book of Mormon, Moroni 8:20-22)

"Behold I say unto you, that he that supposeth that little children need baptism is in the gall of bitterness and in the bonds of iniquity, for he hath neither faith, hope, nor charity; wherefore, should he be cut off while in the thought, he must go down to hell" (Book of Mormon, Moroni 8:14). And in modern revelation we obtain a further understanding, *"But behold I say unto you, that little children are redeemed from the foundation of the world through mine only begotten: Therefore, they cannot sin, for power is not given unto Satan to tempt little children, until they begin to become accountable before me; for it is given unto them even as I will, according to mine own pleasure, that great things may be required at the hands of their fathers"* (Doctrine & Covenants 29: 46-48).

The Latter Day Saints teach that through modern day revelation the Lord has revealed that personal accountability commences at the age of eight years old and therefore all children are to be baptized at the age of eight (Doctrine & Covenants 68:27).

At the time this divine instruction was given the Lord further admonished the Latter Day Saints, to teach their children the doctrine of repentance, faith in Christ, the value of prayer, to keep the Sabbath day holy, and to walk uprightly before the Lord. Apparently an eight year old has the capacity to understand and reason, at least to a certain degree, and therefore, commences at that age to be accountable for his own conduct. Parents are further counseled. that those who fail to so teach their children, *"the sin be upon the heads of the parents"* (Doctrine & Covenants 68:25).

Gift of the Holy Ghost

Baptism is not a complete ordinance without the laying on of hands for the gift of the Holy Ghost. *"Except a man <u>be born of water and of the spirit</u> he cannot enter into the Kingdom of God"* (John 3:5). We have discussed being born of the water, which is baptism, but what is being born of the spirit? John the Baptist declared, *"I indeed baptize you with water unto repentance; but he that cometh after me is mightier than I, whose shoes I am not worthy to bear: He shall baptize you with the Holy Ghost and with fire"* (Matthew 3:11).

The person John had reference to was Christ who bore the Melchizedek Priesthood, (Hebrews 5:10), which priesthood has the power to bestow the Gift of the Holy Ghost, because it is the power over things spiritual as well as things temporal. John the Baptist held the Aaronic Priesthood, the Priesthood after the order of Aaron, which has power to administer to temporal things but not spiritual.

The early Apostles received the Melchizedek Priesthood under the hands of Christ and exercised it to bestow the Gift of the Holy Ghost upon candidates who were worthy. *"Now when the apostles which were at Jerusalem heard that Samaria had received the word of God, they sent unto them Peter and John; who when they were come down, prayed for them, that they might receive the Holy Ghost: (for as yet he was fallen upon none of them; only they were baptized in the name of the Lord Jesus). Then laid they there hands on them, and they received the Holy Ghost"* (Acts 8:14–17).

To be *"born of the spirit"*, is to receive the Gift of the Holy Ghost by the laying on of hands by one who has authority.

The object and purpose of this great gift, is to provide a newly baptized soul with the means of learning the truth, and thereby developing a strong and abiding faith and testimony of the Lord Jesus Christ and Him crucified. (see note 3 at the end of this chapter).

The Holy Ghost is the third member of the God Head who has the express calling of teaching, comforting, and bearing witness of the truth. As Christ prepared His Apostles prior to His crucifixion and told them He would leave them, He also promised them another comforter. *"But the comforter which is the Holy Ghost, whom the Father will send in my name, he shall teach you all things, and bring all things to your remembrance, whatsoever I have said unto you"* (John 14:26). And again, *"But when the comforter is come whom I will send unto you from the Father, even the spirit of truth which proceeded from the Father, he shall testify of me"* (John 15:26).

Then again, the Lord referring to the Holy Ghost as the spirit of truth stated: *"He shall guide you into all truth: for he shall not speak of himself; but whatsoever he shall hear, that shall he speak: and he will show you things to come"* (John 16:13).

To teach, bear witness, comfort in pain and anguish, reveal things of the future are clearly the duties of the Holy Ghost; and no man can know the truth of the scriptures nor comprehend the breadth, nor the depth of them except by and through the Gift of the Holy Ghost. And no man can receive the Gift of the Holy Ghost except he follow the formula prescribed by Peter on the day of Pentecost.

On that memorable day Peter bore witness to about 3000 Jews that the very same Jesus whom they had crucified was the Messiah they had awaited for centuries. And the minds of these 3000 Jews were opened by the spirit of truth and they perceived that the apostles spoke the truth. *"Now when they heard this they were pricked in their hearts, and said unto Peter and the rest of the Apostles, men and brethren, what shall we do? Then Peter said unto them, repent, and be baptized every one of you in the name of Jesus Christ for the remission of sins, and ye shall receive the Gift of the Holy Ghost. For the promise is unto you, and to your children, and to all that are afar off, even as many as the Lord our God shall call"* (Acts 2:36-41).

These 3000 Jews have just learned that they had participated in the killing of their long awaited Messiah, and being racked with guilt asked *"what shall we do"*. Then Peter, the chief apostle, revealed to them what they could do to start the process of forgiveness. Repent, and be baptized by immersion by one who has authority and receive the Gift of the Holy Ghost . . . . and may I add endure to the end . . . . is the formula for admittance to the Kingdom of God. This formula does not guarantee salvation. However, it does provide the honest in heart with the candidacy to strive for salvation which is exaltation in the Celestial Kingdom of God, as discussed in our last chapter.

Our next subject, ... works, is further amplification of the expectation of the Lord of you and I as He counseled in the sermon on the mount. *"Ask, and it shall be given you; seek, and ye shall find; knock, and it shall be opened unto you: For every one that asketh receiveth; and he that seeketh findeth; and to him that knocketh it shall be opened"* (Matthew 7: 7-8). Ask, seek, knock are all words that imply effort on our part. Action that requires works. This scripture is, really a commandment from the Lord, with a promise . . . . *"he that asks receives, he that seeketh will find, and he that knocketh, to him it shall be opened"*; the reward for faithful works is always followed by divine confirmation.

NOTE 3

In speaking of the Holy Ghost, the scriptures tell us, *"Even the spirit of truth; whom the world cannot receive because it seeth him not . . . .",* (John 14:17). The world, the majority of mankind, will never experience the touch of the Holy Ghost simply because they can't see him. What a sad commentary on the world of man. I have heard people say, "I only believe what I can see". This is naïve at best and boarders on stupidity at worst. In point of fact the unseen world, the microscopic world, and the telescopic world is much larger than our own. And neither of these worlds are casually seen, ... one because it is so small and the other because it is so huge and vast.

It is remarkable to me that the majority of the people in the world will not receive, or seek the Holy Ghost, because they can't see him. The real point is they won't make the effort to reccive him. The Holy Ghost is a perfect gentleman and will not come where he is not wanted, ... he is not intrusive. He must respect our agency. However he will meet the honest investigator more than half way.

The Holy Ghost is a gift of enormous spiritual access and insight and is given to newly baptized members of the Church, to facilitate their spiritual growth and development. However this powerful entity will bear witness to investigators, those who are seeking the truth as in the case of Cornelious, the Roman Centurian, spoken of in Acts 10. Cornelious was probably the first gentile to receive the Gospel in the meridian of time. His experience demonstrates that the Holy Ghost will facilitate conversion of the honest in heart, prior to baptism.

Now let me suggest how the Holy Ghost operates. If, as you have read these chapters, and your feelings have been stirred by what you are reading, ... if it "feels", like a "familiar voice", and your interest has been piqued, ... you have been touched, ... softly, by the Holy Ghost. If it sounds logical! These feelings will continue if you read with a prayer in your heart and with real intent. The "influence", of the Holy Ghost may be experienced as a feeling of truth, leading one to exclaim, "Yes I see it now". Or the feelings can be very powerful causing joy unspeakable, frequently manifested as, "tears of joy".

This investigative effort of "real intent', is very key. The Holy Ghost being a spirit, can and will communicate with our spirit (see note 1). However having the capacity to know our thoughts, through our spirits, he will only respond to "real intent".

Our mouths, our eyes, the shrug of a shoulder, in fact our body language, by which we communicate outwardly, can be very deceptive and send any signal we wish, ... to our family, friends and neighbors . . . . but our spirits cannot deceive. The only beings who know our inner most thoughts are the Godhead, and of course those to whom we reveal them. These thoughts, for better or worst, will be revealed, in the court of last resort, when we stand before the judgment bar of God. As long as we are in the flesh these thoughts can be altered or even expunged by sincere repentance, before that awesome day. Of course we can, and are encouraged to measure our thoughts and deeds against the yard stick of the Gospel of Jesus Christ, ... the standard of divine expectation, on a daily basis, and make course corrections as prompted by the Holy Ghost.

The Case for Works

I had always thought, even as a boy that good works were a part of being a good Christian. You know, live a good life, think good thoughts, and if you strayed off course get on your knees and ask God for forgiveness. I still believe this principle of good works.

However, as I got out into the world and had doctrinal exchanges with other Christians, I discovered that the bulk of Christendom consider works to be unnecessary for individual salvation. Yes, I learned that one need only accept Jesus as their Savior. This, as I am told, comes from the belief that since Jesus has died for our sins, if we claim Him as our Savior, and proclaim that we are born again our sins are absolved. In fact, if we maintain that works (forsaking our sins), are necessary for salvation we deny His suffering on the cross in our behalf.

Such Christians maintain that they are saved. Which is to say that they have escaped any and all punishment for their sins done in the flesh. If all you do is accept Jesus then . . . . immediately the probationary test of mortality is over, and almost nothing you do from then on, short of murder, changes your saved position before God.

It occurs to me that this is a very convenient philosophy of right and wrong, and one has to wonder, if gaining salvation is really that easy?

It's truly amazing to me how any reasonably intelligent human being can seriously believe that God would permit His beloved Son, His only begotten Son in the flesh, who was sinless, the only perfect man, ... to suffer, bleed, and die in excruciating agony, in order that any of us can believe and do anything we want just as long as we accept Him as our Savior.

I don't think this is what Jesus had in mind when He said, ... *"If Ye love me keep my commandments"* (John 14: 15). Any one would be foolish indeed, to think they could please the Lord in any other way than by keeping His commandments, *"He that saith, I know him, and keepeth not his commandments, is a liar and the truth is not in him"* (1 John 2:3-6).

In order to make the effort to keep the Lords commandments, one must have faith that He lives, that He is omnipotent, and that He will reward those who are willing to make the effort to keep His commandments.

Does it just take a walk down the isle in response to the invitation of a preacher, to the alter and "stand up for Jesus" and for ever there after declaring, "I love the Lord, I am saved", in order to be saved? Or does it take a life time of making the sacrifice to deny our sins, keep all of His commandments, and endure to the end, in the hope of life eternal?

What are the chances that a disciple who kept all the commandments of God all his life might be rejected, in the final judgment, and one who stood up in church declared for Jesus and lived riotously the rest of his life would be accepted in the final judgment. Is this the Lords expectation of the modern Christian?

I think people who believe that works are not necessary have put the cart before the horse.

They believe they are saved and guaranteed salvation in heaven and their conduct for the rest of their mortal life has no bearing on their saved position.

James was much closer to the mark when he declared, *"Thou believest that there is one God; thou doest well: the Devils also believe and tremble. But wilt thou know, O vain man, that faith without works is dead"* (James 2:19-20). According to James, faith isn't faith with out works.

Luke the physician also records, (Luke 11:9), *"And I say unto you, ask, and it shall be given you; seek and ye shall find; knock and it will be opened unto you"*. Ask, seek and knock, all action words that imply effort at an individual level, that suggest that we are to be active participants in this very important endeavor and not merely spectators. To put forth effort suggests motivation of some kind, for some reason.

The point being the creature must make the effort to know the creator, and to be known of Him. In other words put forth works to demonstrate ones integrity. And we have learned by observation of Apostles and Prophets that such effort must be sincere, even to the point of sacrifice if necessary.

Our God is a jealous God, He is a very, very detailed God, and He only accepts works done His way. However, He is a giver of outstanding gifts, to those who love Him and keep His commandments.

Okay, then all of you who believe in works answer this question!

If in our life time we keep all of His commandments, and endure to the end, will we be saved? Will we have succeeded in earning salvation?

Probably not, we may still fall short. (see Luke 17: 6-10). Here the Lord instructs that if we only do our duty, as Christians, we are still unprofitable servants.

A corollary to Luke 17:6-10, is the college student, who at the beginning of the semester is told by his professor that if he attends all classes, reads all assignments, passes all test, the best grade he can get is a C. Because in order to get a B or an A one must do much more. Such as write a 40 page thesis on an approved subject, with applicable references and foot notes, diagrams, pictures, lab test results, etc. Get the picture? One must do a lot more work.

But then Jesus will say to that faithful disciple . . . . my grace is sufficient for you . . . . so on judgment day His grace will save the struggling disciple. And why? Because the effort made was honest and courageous and the intent of the disciples heart was right before the Lord, ... it was a good faith effort.

Isn't this the <u>hope</u> of the Christian? That after all his good works, after his best effort through out his life he will be found worthy to receive of the grace of God, and be judged worthy to hear *"well done thou good and faithful servant, enter into the rest of the Lord"*.

So I would say with James, *"I will show you my faith by my works"* (James 2: 17-18).

Wait a minute one may ask? That's all well and good, but Didn't Jesus die for our sins, didn't He perform the infinite atonement and take upon Himself our sins?

The answer is yes of course He did, and the atonement accomplished two wonderful things.

<u>First</u> it accomplished the resurrection. All mortals, even the Adolph Hitler's of the world will be resurrected. This is a free gift given to every mortal. Not only will everyone be resurrected but they will be beautiful people as far as appearance is concerned. All of the corruption of the flesh will be removed. Paul understood this principle and taught the Corinthians *"For since by man came death,*

*by man came also the resurrection of the dead. For as in Adam all die,
even so in Christ shall all be made alive"* (1 Corinthinans 15: 21-22).

Second, the other part of the atonement is also associated with
the great pain this perfect man, Jesus Christ, experienced in the
Garden of Gethsemane. Here He took upon himself the sins of all
mankind, for all past, present and future generations, for billions
and billions of souls. I have no idea how He accomplished this, but
the record bears witness that the pain He suffered was so intense,
so grievous . . . . as to cause Him, ... a perfect man, ... a
God, ... to bleed at every pore of His body because of pain.

Now what was the purpose of the second part of the atonement?
The purpose was to reconcile fallen man to God. And to over
come the effects of the "Fall".

Perhaps a little review of the "Fall" as discussed in chapter 5
would be useful at this point.

Adam as the representative of the entire world of mortal man
willfully transgressed a law to fulfill a higher law and was cast
out of the presence of God. Being cast out of the presence of God
is a spiritual death. We call this "the fall ". And from that point
on men were consigned to forever be estranged from God and in
the grasp of Satan (sin).

When Adam and Eve were originally placed in the garden of
Eden, the scriptures tell us that they were subject to conditions
that do not apply to mortal man. They were immortal. They
couldn't die, until they ate the forbidden fruit. Also Adam and Eve
were with out sin. Until they partook of the tree of the knowledge
of good and evil they didn't have the knowledge necessary to
commit sin.

However when they partook of the fruit of the tree of knowledge they became "wise" and they became mortal and therefore subject to death by old age. This is a physical death.

Then as a result of their transgression they were cast out of the presence of God, This constitutes a spiritual death and the "fall".

As the Lord of the earth, Adams actions brought the judgments pronounced on he and Eve upon on all flesh. Men and animal. In their fallen state the children that Adam and Eve bore are all mortal, and they are all subject to grow old and die, and they are destined to remain forever ostracized (rejected) from the presence of God; . . . . because man of his own free will intentionally transgressed a law of God, the law of justice demanded that man be cast out of the presence of God . . . . a spritual death.

The whole point of the second part of the atonement is to overcome the effects of the spiritual death of man and thereby provide mankind a way back into the presence of God; through the law of mercy. Since all mankind were subject to the fall and since all men are sinners, only a sinless man . . . . one over whom Satan had no power, could accomplish the atonement. And Jesus Christ, the Lord omnipotent, was that Man.

So then the mortal death, of man is, resolved by the resurrection of the Lord, a free gift to every mortal. The spiritual death is also resolved but only on certain conditions, as set forth in the second part of the atonement. Resolution of this second death is not a free gift, to man, as is the resurrection.

In part 2 of the atonement Jesus pays the price for this willful act by man (Adam) on the condition that man will accept the sacrifice accomplished by the Lord Jesus Christ.

Since man of his own free will left the presence of God then man of his own free will must make the effort to qualify to come back into the presence of God. If the effort that man makes is deemed by the Lord to be a good faith effort then the Lord will reward him with the portion of grace necessary to qualify the man to enter Gods presence.

Paul, in commenting on this, great sacrifice, has declared, *"He is the author of Eternal Salvation, to all who obey him"* (Heb 5:9). Since the resurrection is a free gift, and therefore requires no obedience on our part Paul in this scripture is talking about the effort required to come back into the presence of God.

If one believes Paul, Jesus is not the author of eternal salvation to those who profess their belief in Him but ignore His laws, ... but rather Jesus, is the author of eternal salvation to all those who *"<u>obey him.</u>"*

Why one may ask? In order that we can qualify to come back into the presence of God the Eternal Father. But what are we to obey? We are to obey laws of behavior that Jesus knows will change our nature and qualify us to prepare to come back into the presence of God the Father. He and His chosen oracles call these laws, "The Gospel of Jesus Christ".

I understand that the saved by grace only people, believe that to presume to have to live by a set of gospel laws diminishes what Jesus did for us on the cross. So refusing to follow the plan that Jesus has defined, they do not subscribe to the Lords plan of salvation and thereby become a <u>law unto themselves,</u> and as such cannot qualify under part 2 of the atonement. Why? Because if a man does not repent and come unto Christ, the Redeemer, and do the works He requires, that man is not redeemed from the fall and remains subject to the buffetings of Satan (Hell).

John tells us that all men have sinned (1 John 1: 8-10). How then can anyone possibly qualify for part 2 of the atonement? We can't fully. Not without a lot of divine help in mortality and also on judgment day, and then only if we prove worthy to receive that help.

That introduces us to another very important "work" of the Gospel, ... called repentance. Jesus knows the thoughts of our minds and the intent of our hearts, and only sincere repentance is acceptable to Him. Not only must we sincerely ask for forgiveness, but we must forsake our sins. One of the tasks of the truly penitent is to never return to the sin for which one has earnestly sought forgiveness. Because we are sinners and live in a world full of sin, this can be a life time effort, and probably will be.

And the reality of the faithful disciple is that he will try his best each and every day to please the Lord he loves, and in the process, little by little, he will begin to live laws that are more closely aligned with the expectation of Christ.

In the repentance process we draw closer to Christ we get to know Him better . . . . this association with Jesus through repentance . . . . increases our trust in the Lord; and leads to deep respect, appreciation and love for the Lord.

As a result the disciple will start to live Celestial laws. And, in time, ... any other kind of life will become foreign and uncomfortable to him.

I have talked about the Lords plan of salvation, but what is it?

The principles of this plan were preached by Peter on the day of Pentacost as recorded in Acts 2:37-41. Here we read that his listeners, about 3000 souls, had just been convinced, by Peters preaching, that they had killed their Messiah and they were, *"pricked in their hearts"*, and moved to action to ask, *"men and brothers what can we do"?* Here they experienced the beginnings of faith. And Peter answered, *"repent and be baptized by immersion for the remission of sins, and receive the Gift of the Holy ghost".*

Peters formula, demonstrated by this scripture, shows that the first principle of the plan of salvation is . . . . faith. The 3000 had been pricked in their hearts and moved to ask . . . . *"what can we do"?* These 3000 believed what Peter told them. They had faith. Then Peter tells then . . . . *"repent and be baptized by immersion, and then receive the Holy Ghost".*

The second principle is repent. The third principle, sees the investigator baptized and washed clean of sin. This now washed clean investigator receives the gift of the Holy Ghost by the laying on of hands by the apostle of the Lord . . . . or their designee; which is the fourth principle of the plan of salvation. There is a fifth principle . . . . that is perhaps the most difficult of all and that is . . . . to endure to the end.

What then is the basic tenet behind "the saved by grace only" philosophy, of so many, many people. This has been discussed earlier in this chapter, however; I understand that a basis for this belief is scripture such as that found in the writings of the Apostle Paul. For example, in his letter to the Ephesians 2: 8, Paul declares, *"For by Grace are ye saved through faith and that not of yourselves: it is the gift of God".* He continues in verse 9, *"Not of works lest any man should boast".*

As a works enthusiast by choice I see several things in these scriptures, basically because I understand them in the context of all of the rest of the scriptures and not as stand alone scriptures. Lets review them:

<u>Tenet</u>: *"For by Grace are ye saved through faith".*

What does this scripture say to me?: It says blessings of grace from the Lord comes as a free gift, only after we have done all we can to qualify for eternal life and He is pleased with the effort we have made.

<u>Tenet</u>: *"Not of works lest any man should boast".*

What does this scripture mean to me? No man, however valiant, on judgment day will be able to say, "I did it myself". I believe that Paul is saying that man is incapable of saving himself no matter how hard he tries. However, Christ will reward the effort that He judges to be valiant, with His grace. That sounds reasonable . . . . He paid for the right to judge all men.

To really understand Paul's position regarding these two scriptures we should also review the very next scripture, Eph 2:10. *"For we are his workmanship, created in Jesus <u>unto good works</u>, which God hath before ordained that we should walk in them".*

Let me tell you what I think this scripture is saying:

Jesus is the Creator of this world, and is the author of the plan of salvation, because of His atonement, ... a plan that God the Father endorsed before the world was created. A plan that will over come the fall and bring us back into His presence, if we perform the required works. Works that God knows are within our ability to perform.

This last scripture makes it obvious that Paul had no intention of diminishing the value of works as a basis, for eternal salvation, and his discussion on grace, shows the mercy of Christ that will be extended to those who are judged to have been valiant throughout their life.

Paul was himself a tireless worker from the time of his conversion. However, I submit that even Paul, this valiant Apostle, needed and received the grace of Christ for his own salvation. Wasn't he a persecutor of the Christians before his miraculous conversion, causing many to be thrown in jail? He even took part in the martyrdom of Steven, and after his conversion and because of it apparently had such profound feelings of guilt that he considered himself to be the least of the apostles, and not worthy to be an apostle at all.

Peter too, the Chief apostle, denied Jesus, not once but three times, and spent the rest of his life trying to put that act behind him. These men as valiant as they were and as work oriented still needed the grace of Jesus, to achieve salvation. (See note 4 at the end of this chapter).

So at this point let me summarize my position . . . . The work oriented group of which I am one, believes that we are ultimately also saved by grace. However unlike the "saved by grace only" people, the work oriented group believes that through a life time of repentance and good works one can qualify to become a <u>candidate</u> to be saved by grace, and a saved determination can only be made by the Lord, because He purchased us with His blood. Therefore the work oriented individual must do the works the Lord and His chosen oracles have defined, all his life in the hope that he qualifies to be saved. This life time effort is called enduring to the end.

Now then the next obvious consideration to both groups is understanding what Faith really is. In this regard the scriptures bear ample testimony that *"faith without works is dead"* (James 2: 14-26). James says, *"as the body without the spirit is dead, so faith without works is dead also"*.

Let me illustrate. Picture a man sitting in a boat on a lake. Lets take a little license with a boat and call it "the good ship faith". On one oar write the word belief, and on the other oar write the word works. Now pull on the oar called belief and what will happen? The boat will go in a circle and not straight ahead. Now just pull on the oar with the word "works". The same thing will happen. One needs to pull both oars in order for progress to be made and the "good ship faith" to move ahead . . . . or for faith to occur.

Faith is a principle of action, (Heb 11:1) based on a belief that a loving Heavenly Father, actually exists, is a rewarder of those who seek Him, and who are being motivated by a strong desire to please Him.

I encourage you to read the entire chapter of Hebrews 11. All forty verses, are a magnificent treatise on examples through out history of people who accomplished great works because of their faith in an unseen God, and the realization that they would be blessed for their effort.

So dear reader you be the judge . . . . what is the best course of action for you? It's your agency use it wisely. As for me I remain a worker. Jesus was a worker . . . I am in very good company.

And I believe that those who feel as I do are a minority in the Christian world. And this is sad to me in consideration of the scripture in Matthew 7: 13-14, where we read of the Lords prophesy concerning the "majority", *"Enter ye in at the strait gate: for wide is the gate and broad is the way, that leadeth to destruction, and many their be which go in thereat: Because strait is the gate and narrow is the way, which leadeth unto life, and few there be that find it".* This scripture is a prophetic declaration by the Lord as to what will happen to the inhabitants of the earth. Certainly, it does not bode well for the majority.

Some time ago an elitist fringe element of the saved by grace only crowd departed even further from the truth as seen in the article quoted as follows:

The Tacoma News Tribune, dated Friday Feb 25, 1994, reported on a story by Mary Rourke, of the Los Angeles Times, that in a meeting of 74 Christian bible scholars, at a think tank at the Westar Institute, in Sonoma, Calif, they reached consensus by a vote summarized, as follows:

*   The Jesus that most people know is a myth.
*   Mary was not a virgin
*   Jesus was born in Nazareth, not Bethlehem, and the nativity story is pure fantasy.
*   Jesus didn't teach the Lord's prayer.
*   He didn't preach the sermon on the mount.
*   He didn't raise anyone from the dead.
*   Jesus said just 18% of the things attributed to Him.

Apparently these "bible scholars" are attempting to, humanize Jesus. In the process they have stripped Him of His divinity. And in this effort they have been carefully led by Satan and unbeknownst to themselves have become anti-Christ. Truly the wisdom of the wise is foolishness (1 Corinthians 3:19-20)

So, in summary, the Atonement part 1 is applicable to all mortals, we will all be beautiful people, and part 2 is applicable only to the "few" who exercise faith unto repentance, and endure in good works to the end, or in other words, who are valiant in the testimony of Jesus.

Another hall mark of the "saved by grace only" crowd is the belief that the heavens are sealed, and that God no longer speaks to man, and doesn't need to because we have a bible. The bible is a history of Gods revelations to mortals through chosen oracles

(Apostles and Prophets) to teach man what they must do to return to God, and to certify the Lord Jesus Christ as the redeemer of the world.

The bible, or compilation of revelatory writings, was given to an ancient people who needed them for guidance in their lives, and in their time. This fact, in no way diminishes the bible as timeless in its application and usefulness to our time, as well, for guidance and for reproof.

To illustrate: If to ancient Israel it was the penalty of death if they broke the Sabbath (Exodus 31:14-15), then it certainly would behoove us in our time to take heed and keep the Sabbath day holy. If, in Moses day, a man was stoned to death for committing adultery (Leviticus:20:10), then we certainly are wise enough today not to commit the same sin.

Unless we believe that God only meant that law to be applicable to the ancient Israelites. But to our more enlightened generation that law isn't applicable, because Jesus has since come and paid the price for our sins. And since we have accepted Him, as our savior, we are not under the law, and we can then commit these same sins without concern for our standing before God?

Think about it. If, God is no respecter of persons and if, He would permit the taking of the life of an ancient Israelite for breaking the Sabbath or committing adultery, will He really hold us guiltless for these same infractions of the law? I am sure this entire nation lies under righteous condemnation for these infractions of the law and in Gods due time will be called to account.

Make no mistake; the atonement is applicable to ALL men; not just those who lived after the time of the Garden of Gethsemane, or the cross.

The Gospel of Jesus Christ, replaces the law of Moses and is even more restrictive and demanding than the law of Moses. The law of Moses was given to ancient Israel, and served a people who were in bondage to Egyptian masters for 400 years who, in time, lost the capability of self government and became little more than beasts of burden.

The Gospel, of the new testament, was given to a people who had developed the capability of self government, people who lived in the meridian of time.

For example, the law of Moses said, *"Thou shalt not commit adultery"*, where as the Gospel directs that, *"if a man looketh upon a women with lust in his heart he is guilty of adultery"* (Matthew 5:28). This is a huge change. To be as guilty of thinking an act as one would be if he actually did it. The Lord expects much more of people who live under the laws of the Gospel of Jesus Christ.

If the bible was written to an ancient people, where is modern mans revelations from God? According to the modern Christian the bible is the only prevailing word of God to modern man. So we must be able to conclude that God must feel we are so enlightened and perfect that we don't need His guidance . . . . or the Christian world is wrong, and we desperately need divine guidance in our day.

The scriptures tell us that God *"is no respecter of persons"* (Acts 10:34), meaning He is equally concerned about all of us in all generations of time. In the light of this scripture consider this thought. God rained down fire and brimstone on the great plains cities of Sodom and Gomorrah, because their sensual sins were so grievous and pervasive. And yet much of our present day world is obsessed with sensual gratification, and perversion of the powers of procreation is rampant.

The same sins that brought down fire from Heaven, on Sodom and Gomorrah exist in our modern world. In fact, laws are being passed to protect many who use their God given powers of procreation to do that which is unnatural. The daily news regales us with acts of moral depravity that seem to know no bounds. If ever a world needed guidance from God our modern day Sodom and Gomorrah does.

But God will not speak to a people who believe He is a mute, except it be to their condemnation.

However the saved by grace only crowd, don't follow the bible, the wisdom that they obtained from the Jews. The modern Christian wouldn't have a bible if it were not for the Jews. What then does the bible really mean to modern day Christianity? I am afraid not very much.

Some years ago as a missionary I was invited to speak to a youth group of a very large Christian church in the University district near the University of Washington. After my talk and a brief question and answer period, the leader of this group commented, *"I am surprised that you Mormons take the bible so literally, everyone knows much of it is just folklore"*.

I disagree with that assessment. The bible is a witness of the divinity of the Lord Jesus Christ, and contains wisdom that is timeless, and excellent for reproof and guidance, and while our generation can benefit from the bible . . . . where is our revelation from God? Revelation that is applicable and unique to our day? It is not to be found, except in a Church ". . . . *with a foundation of Apostles and Prophets"* (Ephesians 2:20).

Works are the very back bone of true Christianity. But words and thoughts, powers of persuasion, use of logic are all of no consequence in achieving true understanding, unless the reader

Louis A. Kelsch

becomes a participant. Only then will the God of Heaven respond and touch the willing heart with His spirit.

As Paul declared, *"I have planted, Apollo's watered; but God gave the increase"* (1 Corinthians 3:6). The things of God are spiritually discerned and are only revealed to the honest in heart. The secrets of God are hidden from the natural man, hence *"narrow is the way that leads to life eternal and few their be that find it"*. I hope and pray that you find it.

NOTE 4

The grace I am speaking of here is that grace necessary to qualify one for salvation in the Kingdom of Heaven. Apparently the Lord will extend His saving grace to a worthy disciple anytime He wishes. For example Paul in 2 Corinthians 12:2-6, speaks of being lifted up to the third Heaven (Celestial Glory) and saw and heard things that were unspeakable, and not lawful to be uttered. It would appear that he was so valiant that in his fourteenth year as an Apostle of the Lord he was translated and taken up to Heaven where the Lord revealed to him marvelous truths and understanding, but forbade him to reveal them. And in Matthew 17:1-9, Peter, James and John are taken by the Lord up to the mountain where the Lord was transfigured before them and appeared before them in His glory, *"and his face did shine as the sun, and his raiment was white as the light"*, they also saw Moses and Elias (Elijah). They were commanded to tell the visions they had seen to no man until after the Lords crucifixion. These men were privileged to have redeeming revelations.

I would assume that anyone could experience similar such magnificent revelations, in manifestations of grace, if they do the works that Paul and Peter did.

The scriptures are full of spiritual manifestations made to deserving mortals, as the Lord extends His grace. It would appear that this is done for the purpose of testimony building, for conversion, for strength to over come evil, and as a witness of truth. In this manner the Lord acting, most often through the Holy Ghost, will carefully lead the honest disciple, adding grace upon grace and virtue upon virtue here a little and there a little until the perfect day.

Louis A. Kelsch

However, the gifts of saving grace from the Lord, come in His way and His time. After all they are His gifts, and must be obtained His way. (See the chapter on, First Principles of the gospel . . . . for His way).

The Scriptures

The purpose of this chapter is to illustrate the burden of the scriptures in the King James version (KJV) of the Holy Bible, the Book of Mormon (B/M), the Doctrine and Covenants (D/C) and the Pearl of Great Price (P of GP). The object of these inspired records is to define the effort required, by us mortals, to succeed in this second or mortal estate.

As I have learned over the years, the purpose for all scripture is first to testify to the divinity of the Lord Jesus Christ, and second for reproof or guidance emanating from a far, far superior intelligence, than mans, on how to best live our lives in mortality in order to qualify for eternal life.

Apparently this omnipotent entity known as God wants us to have the most excellent opportunity possible in this mortal experience and to return to Him, after our life is over.

And it, also seems these expectations are centered around rules, of behavior, that He knows will work. He chooses to call these, rules of behavior, scriptures.

Rules of behavior suggest that interested people will orient their conduct to conform to these rules because of trust and respect for this God.

I call the desire or motivation to conform belief, and the effort to conform, works; both of which, working together, constitute . . . . faith.

Belief and works are necessary to demonstrate our love for the Lord and to qualify for, and then remain in the warm certitude (the grace) of the redemptive powers of the atonement wrought by the Lord Jesus Christ.

The scriptures contain and reveal the purposes, and objectives of God pertinent to the mortal life of man. Through the years, the scriptures, have been the basis for the formation of laws of civilized societies.

The scriptures are the original basis of the standards used in the courts of the land, to judge individual behavior.

Scriptures literally are the standard, or the bench mark, of truth and therefore the measuring idiom of all mortal thought and behavior.

The latter day saints designate as scripture, *"that which is spoken under the influence of the Holy Ghost"* (Bible dictionary page 770).

Prophets of God and other chosen oracles, such as Apostles, either kept or caused records to be kept of things they were told by revelation, as in the case of Old Testament records: or as they observed or were told first hand by the Lord; or as were written to congregations under the influence of the Holy Ghost as in the case of New Testament records. And in all cases the records are scripture.

Scriptures provide inspiration. I have personally found that the scriptures are blessed with a spiritual dimension, that is hard to quantify but, is very real. For example if the reader is reading with prayerful intent, with faith in God, the scriptures will be a source of excitement, and the reader will experience a conviction of truth, and the thrill of discovery. This experience can be life changing.

On the other hand if one reads as an intellect, with reservation, as one not yet willing to embrace, then this spiritual dimension, and a conviction of truth may not be experienced.

And as I read the scriptures I am impressed with the spirit and the power of the instruction which is designed to make us better people.

Additionally, the scriptures are to me living documents. By that I mean that subsequent readings inevitably provide insights not seen nor understood in the initial readings. This experience suggests that the reader has experienced spiritual progress. Such spiritual manifestations are known as . . . . adding here a little and their a little . . . . until the perfect day.

The scriptures describe optimum behavior expectations of man by the Creator of this world.

They are in fact a compilation of laws that if conscientiously applied produce character traits that qualify the participant for eternal life. Which is to live eternally in Gods presence.

As you read the scriptures it becomes very clear that works based on the lessons of obedience and sacrifice is the purpose of our existence. It becomes apparent that works is the very essence of true Christianity.

Now in consideration of the scriptures known as the King James version of the Holy Bible, particularly those of the new testament, I would ask? To whom were these laws given? The answer is, they were given to members of the Church of Jesus Christ of <u>Meridian Day Saints</u>, in the form of preaching, or letters to congregations from ordained Apostles. (see note 5, for explanation of the term "Saints", at the end of this chapter.)

They were given to those who were Jews, of the house of Israel and later to the gentiles who were, *"no more strangers and foreigners but fellow citizens with the saints and of the household of God"*. Who, *"are built upon a foundation of Apostles and Prophets"* (Eph 2:19-22).

These Apostalic letters were given to a people who had been baptized by immersion for the remission of sins and had hands laid upon their heads, by those who held the priesthood authority, for the gift of the Holy Ghost. Which gift *"shall teach you all things, and bring all things to your remembrance"*, but *"whom the world cannot receive because it seeth him not"* (John 14:16-26).

Apparently the bulk of humanity will never receive the Holy Ghost because, for whatever reason, they will not make the effort to develop the spiritual sensitivity to feel his presence. One can only "see" the Holy Ghost through the eye's of faith.

However, this third member of the Godhead, the Holy Ghost, has the power to *teach* and *bring all things to remembrance* to those with whom he will communicate.

The Apostle Paul's epistles were written to congregations that Paul and fellow missionaries had converted and baptized and given them the gift of the Holy Ghost, by the laying on of hands (Acts 8: 14-17).

These congregations understood what Paul was saying. They knew him, his way of preaching, his mannerisms, his body language, his passions, his love for the Lord. They knew the sound of his voice.

Not long ago I heard a TV preacher reciting some of these same scriptures in Ephesians and declaring to the audience, *"and what did Paul tell us."* And I thought, ... Paul didn't tell you anything, ... he wrote to the Ephesians, members of the Church. Why does that matter?

Because baptized members of the Church also have the Gift of the Holy Ghost to give them understanding (John 14: 26). They were not confounded by the writings of Paul that in our day have produced so much division and even many churches.

In consideration of hundreds of Churches, interestingly enough on, 11 July 2007, the local paper, the Tacoma News Tribune, published a front page article entitled, *"Vatican lays claim to only true church"*. Apparently Pope Benedict XVI, released an article 7/10/07, that says, *"other Christian communities are either defective or not true churches and that Catholicism provides the only true path to salvation"*.

Sounds very much like a Catholic condemnation of all protestant churches.

This puts me in mind of a quote I read many years ago in a book entitled, *"A Marvelous Work and A Wonder"*, by Legrand Richards, and on page 3 of the book, is this quote as follows: In a pamphlet entitled, *"The Strength of the Mormon Position"*, the late Elder Orson F Whitney, of the council of the twelve apostles of The Church of Jesus Christ of Latter Day Saints, related the following incident under the heading, *"A Catholic Utterance"*.

"Many years ago a learned man, a member of the Roman Catholic Church, came to Utah and spoke from the stand of the Salt Lake tabernacle. I became well-acquainted with him and we conversed freely and frankly. A great scholar, with perhaps a dozen languages at his tongue's end, he seemed to know all about theology, law, literature, science and philosophy. One day he said to me, "You Mormons are all ignoramuses. You don't even know the strength of your own position. It is so strong that there is only one other tenable in the whole Christian world, and it is the position

of the Catholic Church. If we are right, you are wrong; if you are right we are wrong; and that's all there is to it. The Protestants haven't a leg to stand on. For if we are wrong they are wrong with us, since they were part of us and went out from us; while if we are right they are apostates whom we cut off long ago. If we have the Apostolic succession from Peter, as we claim, there is no need of Joseph Smith and Mormonism; but if we have not that succession then such a man as Joseph Smith was necessary, and Mormonism's attitude is the only consistent one. It is either the perpetuation of the gospel from ancient times, or the restoration of the gospel in latter days".

Why did this catholic scholar make such a statement about the Mormons? Because the Mormons . . . . The Church of Jesus Christ of Latter Day Saints is not a protestant church (See the chapter on Apostasy and Restoration).

And as I reflect on the Mormons and the Catholics . . . . only the Mormons have a foundation of Apostles and Prophets, and can claim and demonstrate continuing revelation. Revelation as evidenced by The Book of Mormon, a companion witness to the bible of the Lord Jesus Christ; the Doctrine and Covenants, a compilation of revelations, received by the Prophet Joseph Smith and other Prophets subsequent to him, from the year 1831 to 1978; for the building up and strengthening of an original American Church. And the Pearl of Great Price, containing detailed accounts of the spiritual and physical creation of the world, and other unique and spiritual writings.

These books plus the King James version of the Holy Bible constitutes the canon of scripture used by the Church of Jesus Christ of Latter Day Saints.

We also consider our monthly magazine publications and weekly Church News to be sources of inspiration and scriptural guidance particularly the compilation of talks given by our General Authorities semi-annually in General Church Conference.

Members of the LDS Church also consider the words spoken by our President of the Church and his counselors, and the quorum of the twelve apostles, to be scripture when spoken under the influence of the Holy Ghost. We sustain these men as Prophets, Seers and Revelators.

My friends if your God is omnipotent then the scriptures, as they exist, are what He considers adequate for us to gain salvation . . . . and can be trusted.

On the other hand; if you consider the scriptures, or any part thereof, to be folklore or myths, your God is not omnipotent . . . . you needn't fear Him or seek succor at His hand.

Through ordained and sustained Prophets Seers and Revelators we, who are members of the Church, have access to divine guidance for our unique times and seasons, in our day. We are not left without divine guidance.

NOTE 5

Through the years the term Saint, has taken on new meaning. Paul through out his epistles refers to the baptized members of the Church as saints. He addresses them as members struggling for perfection.

(i.e.: see Ephesians 4: 11-14, where reference is made "to the perfecting of the Saints") However subsequent to the death of the Apostles and the ensuing apostasy (see chapter 2), the practice crept into the apostate Church; of members, through prayer, partitioning well known and departed saints to intercede with God on their behalf. (1)

This practice was principally, a product of the teachings of Augustine ; the Bishop of Hippo of North Africa, who was the most prolific writer on the subject: that the nature of man is naturally inclined toward evil as a result of the effect of the inherited sin of Adam and Eve, our first parents. Better known as the doctrine of "original sin". (see Durant's "The Age of Faith", page 69, ref: (1). Pg 171.) People in those days were taught that they were so wicked and God so righteous that a known faithful entity was necessary to intercede in their behalf. They lost the truth that Christ was their intercessory with God. John declared, *"Jesus saith unto him, I am the way, the truth, and the life: no man cometh unto the Father, but by me"* (see John 14:6).

To day the Catholic Church holds that certain dead members of that Church who have distinguished themselves through out their lives, and reached what is deemed to be a significant level of notoriety and achievement, in their lifetime, can be canonized and raised to the level of Saint. These canonized entities can then be used for prayer intercessory with God.

This belief and practice is a complete departure from the original Apostolic treatment; and has the net effect of diminishing the role of the Lord Jesus Christ as the only legitimate intercessory with God the Father. In addition the Lords repeated admonition of the rights of the individual to appeal to both Him and our Heavenly Father in prayer was virtually done away with.

We agree with Paul. Saints are mortals who are members of the Church and are working for perfection.

Today, baptized members of the Church of Jesus Christ of Latter Day Saints are referred to as "saints". A "saint" is a person who has committed to God and the world, through baptism by immersion and receipt of the Holy Ghost, by the Laying on of hands by proper authority, that they are working for perfection.

To my knowledge the Church of Jesus Christ of Latter Day Saints is the only Christian Church on planet earth that uses the designation "Saints" in reference to its members.

(1) For an in depth review of the changes that crept into "Christianity" after the apostasy, see "Apostasy to Restoration" by T. Edgar Lyons

Plan of Salvation

Where we came from, why we are here, and where we are going are the subjects of consideration in this chapter.

Pity the soul that sorrowfully lays loved ones to rest, racked with the anguish of their loss, faced with the thought that "lost forever is the sweet association once enjoyed".

When the truth is known, we realize that a plan exists, prepared before the foundations of this world were laid, to provide man with the blessings of continuing endless existence, awareness and association.

In heaven where we lived, before we came to earth and became mortal, we were spirit children (See Romans 8:16) of our heavenly parents, who are immortal. There is a huge difference between spirit people and immortal people. An immortal being as we learned in prior chapters has a glorified body of flesh and bone, (see Luke 24:36-43, when Jesus appeared to His disciples and apostles after His resurrection) and is able to experience great joy, where as a spirit is much more limited in what it can experience and how it can act and be acted upon.

A mortal body and a spirit (the soul) welded together by the resurrection creates an immortal body. Our divine Father wants us to become like Him and to experience the same things He can experience. Don't we as parents want our children to have the blessings we enjoy? . . . . yes and even more. These are natural feelings in the bosom of every concerned parent. And I submit we brought such feelings from Heaven with us as the spirit off spring of our immortal, glorified Father.

In the beginning we lived in Heaven with the eternal Father as His spiritual children. This period of time is called our "first estate". During this estate we were taught under the watchful eye of our Father. Our progression in this estate was very successful and qualified us to be added upon (See Pearl of Great Price, Abraham 3:26).

Having learned all we could, as spirits, it became necessary that other avenues of progression be made available to us.

We needed mortal bodies to progress and we needed the experience of a mortal life to comprehend and partake of the great opportunities the Father has in store for us; and to prove ourselves.

Our Father was anxious for us to progress, so He prepared this world as our second, or mortal estate. This world was to be, in part at least, a prison to us. Oh! not a prison of bars and chains designed to inflict punishment, but a prison serving as a place of confinement. A place where we are consigned to serve a probationary period, in order that we might have the brief experience of a mortality.

This plan to come to earth, and experience mortality, away from the presence of God, our Heavenly Father, was presented to all of us in our first estate by our immortal Father, in a grand council in Heaven (See Job 38:4-7). Many of us, as the spirit children of Heavenly Father, rejoiced at the opportunity to progress and become like Him.

One popular spirit by the name of Lucifer, was not in harmony with our Father's plan and proposed that he be appointed chief executor of a plan that would remove all risk to Father's spirit children. He proposed to send everyone to earth and force them to keep Celestial laws. He would have to admit that his plan would deprive all, of his spirit Brothers and Sisters, of their free agency. Nevertheless, he would bring them all back to the Father and lose none of them.

For his services Lucifer asked for the glory of God that he might be made equal to his divine Father. Lucifer's plan would have returned son's and daughter's to God of whom no father could be proud. Without free agency and the chances to exercise it, the children of God would be little more than mind numbed robots, being oriented to act only as directed; having no power in and of themselves to do or act independently; having no individuality, and therefore being incapable of either receiving or imparting joy and happiness.

Another son stepped forward whose name was Jehovah. He proposed to comply with the will of the Father and send all spirit children to earth. To provide them with free agency and prove them, by their agency, to see if they would do all in their power to perfect themselves and to progress. In order that they might someday come back into the presence of the Father and partake of the joy He has prepared for them.

Jehovah further proposed, if necessary, He would offer His life to provide the children of God a way back into the Father's presence. Jehovah's position in contrast to Lucifer's was unselfish and evidenced love for His spirit brother's and sister's and a humble desire to do the Fathers will. For His services Jehovah wanted no reward, but preferred that all glory and honor belong to the Father, who . . . . indeed, is the true recipient of all glory as the master architect of the plan of salvation from beginning to end.

Needless to say Jehovah was anointed chief executor and was ordained before the earth was created as the Messiah (see 1 Peter1:18-20).

Lucifer was wroth and whipped his followers into open rebellion against God and their was war in Heaven. Here Lucifer using the very agency he was willing to deny his spirit siblings, led a rebellion against God, in company with followers who wanted a risk free mortality. Lucifer and his host, comprising approximately one third (See revelations 12: 7-12) of all the hosts of Heaven, were cast down to the earth as disembodied spirits, having forfeited the possibility of progression by their open rebellion, and that, ... in the very presence of the Father.

Isaiah saw Lucifer's folly and prophetically recorded it thus, for our understanding:

"How art thou fallen from Heaven, O Lucifer, son of the morning! How art thou cut down to the ground, which didst weaken the nations: For thou hast said in thine heart, I will ascend into Heaven, I will exalt my throne above the stars of God: I will sit also upon the mount of the congregation, in the sides of the north: I will ascend above the heights of the clouds, I will be like the most High. Yet thou shalt be brought down to hell, to the sides of the pit. They that see thee shall narrowly look upon thee and consider thee, saying, is this the man that made the earth to tremble that did shake kingdoms" (Isaiah 14:12-16).

When the earth was ready the spirit children of God were sent here in their appointed times and seasons, to acquire bodies of flesh and bones and to learn to prove themselves.

To make certain that we had no alternative but to use our free agency, and learn to make correct choices, our Father wisely placed a veil over our minds blotting out, for our mortal sojourn, all remembrance of our former life in Heaven (see D/C 110:1 and B of M Ether 3:16). This veil only leaves us with about a 10% functioning brain for mortality (So our scientists tell us). However one day, when the veil is removed, we will know what, wonders and accomplishment, is in the other 90%. We will recall . . . . our successes and achievements and associations experienced as spirits in our pre-existence. We will then be able to compare our pre-mortal life with our mortal life at the time of the final judgment.

Such knowledge may cause us great joy or great shame when compared to our mortal memories. This life is the time to prepare to meet God . . . . a time to perform our labors (See Alma 34:32) and to make sure that guilt and shame are not the heritage we leave mortality with.

The disembodied spirits who rebelled in the first estate and were cast out of Heaven, are now, and have been on the earth since the beginning, as devils. Jesus encountered many of these devils during His mission on earth and some very interesting interviews took place in these encounters. Let's investigate several such interviews and analyze them.

"And unclean spirits, when they saw him, fell down before him, and cried, saying Thou art the Son of God, and he straitly charged them that they should not make him known" (Mark 3: 11-12).

"And he healed many that were sick of divers diseases, and cast out many devils; and suffered not the devils to speak, because they knew him" (Mark 1:34).

"And devils also came out of many, crying out: Thou art Christ the Son of God. And he rebuking them suffered them not to speak; for they knew that he was Christ" (Luke 4:41).

The one thing that we observe in these scriptures is that clearly the devils knew Jesus and they knew He was the Son of God. The Jews put Jesus to death for saying He was the Son of God. How did the devils know that Jesus was the Son of God? The answer is simple!

They knew Him from the grand council in Heaven. They knew Him as the mighty Jehovah, the executor of the Father's will. These unclean spirits, had no veil of forgetfulness over their minds as do men in the flesh. They had full and painful recollection of all that happened in the council of Heaven, of their rebellion and subsequent expulsion. Well might they recognize Jesus, and obey Him and promptly too.

This reaction of devils to the presence of Jesus as recorded in holy writ bears powerful and truthful testimony to the divinity of Jesus Christ and to the actuality of a pre-existence.

These scriptures also demonstrate that devils (disembodied spirits) are eager to possess the bodies of their mortal siblings given the opportunity.

As additional evidence of the pre-existence of spirits we read in the bible how Jeremiah was appointed to his mission in mortality, as a prophet, before he was born.

"Then the word of the Lord came unto me, saying, before I formed thee in the belly I knew thee; and before thou camest forth out of the womb I sanctified thee, and I ordained thee a prophet unto the nations" (Jeremiah 1:4-5).

Here Jeremiah was told that he was known of the Lord before he was born and more than that, he was so noble in his first estate that, he was ordained to be a prophet before he was in the womb of his mortal mother.

Like Jeremiah we too lived, in heaven, before we came to earth as mortals. And those of us who were more righteous and didn't rebel as did those who became devils, came to earth to be added upon through the experiences of mortality. And the principle objective of this mortal experience is to teach us obedience (See Hebrews 5:8-9).

In this life we are to learn to purge rebellion, against the commandments of God from our personalities, and through our free agency acquire the desire to do good. There is no place in the Kingdom of Heaven for a rebellious personality as Satan and his hosts have demonstrated; as evidenced by their rebellious behavior in their first estate.

The gospel of Jesus Christ, through the basic tenets of **faith, repentance, baptism by immersion,** and the **laying on of hands for the gift of the Holy Ghost, by proper authority, and enduring to the end** is the pattern of behavior that will prepare us for Eternal Life. These five basic principles constitute the basics of the Lords plan of salvation.

Those who know and understand these things in mortality, are indeed fortunate, because they have access to these tools of salvation. But what happens to those who didn't have the opportunity to hear or learn of the gospel while they were on the earth ? Are they going to have the chance to hear it and accept it or reject it and exercise their agency?

If God is just, and we know that He is, then it would follow that all must have equal opportunity to hear and accept or reject the Gospel of Jesus Christ, ... to make an informed decision. Because to hold out the way of redemption and salvation to some and not to all would be unmerciful. But our Heavenly Father is merciful and has prepared a way whereby all who have not heard the gospel message will have an opportunity. How will this happen?

All spirits when they leave their mortal tabernacles, through death, go to a place called "Spirit World". What do we know about this spirit world?

When Jesus was crucified, two thieves were crucified along with Him. One of the thieves railed on Him and said, *"If thou be Christ save thyself and us"*. But the other thief rebuked the first and said, *"We receive our just rewards, but this man has done nothing amiss"*, then addressing himself to Jesus, he said, *"Lord remember me when thou comest into thy Kingdom"*. Jesus responded to this second thief with the promise, *"Verily I say unto thee: Today shalt thou be with me in Paradise"* (Luke 23: 39-43).

From His own words we know that the Lord's spirit went to a place called Paradise on the day He died and His body was placed in the tomb. Obviously "Paradise" is part of the "Spirit World" because that is where the Lords spirit and the spirit of the thief went on the day they died.

Three days later this same spirit reentered His body and Jesus emerged from the tomb a resurrected man. Jesus first appeared to Mary Magdalena outside of His tomb, and as she hastened to embrace Him, he admonished, *"Touch me not; for I am not yet ascended to my Father: But go to my brethren, and say unto them, I ascend unto my Father, and your Father, and to my God, and to your God"* (John 20:17).

From the foregoing we know that on the day He died on the cross, Jesus went, in the spirit, to a place called Paradise. We also know that three days later when He appeared to Mary outside of His tomb as a resurrected man, He had not as yet been to His Father which is in Heaven. Obviously then Paradise, in the spirit world, and Heaven, where Heavenly Father lives, are not the same place.

What then is Paradise and why did Jesus go there? Peter answered these questions when he declared, *"For Christ also hath once suffered for sins, the just for the unjust, that he might bring us to God, being put to death in the flesh, but quickened by the spirit: By which also he went and preached unto the <u>spirits in Prison</u>"* (1 Peter 3: 18-20), and Peter continues, *"For, for this cause was the gospel preached also to them that are dead, that they might be judged according to man in the flesh but live according to God in the spirit"* (1 Peter 4:6).

In this scripture Peter informed us that in this "spirit world" there is also a "spirit prison" a place of confinement, or a place to be confined until the day of final judgment.

Jesus went to preach to the spirits, of those that are known as dead, that they might be judged according to man in the flesh. Bear in mind that there is no dead with God, only with man. Jesus went to Paradise to establish a Gospel proselyting program, just as He had on earth, in order, to preach the Gospel of salvation to the spirits in the spirit prison.

Spirits in the spirit prison apparently have their agency because they are being *"preached too"* implying an opportunity to make a choice and therefore they have the capacity to accept or reject the gospel . . . . they have agency.

If they accept they can, just as you and I, manifest faith and repentance, but how can they be baptized, and cleansed of their sins since this ordinance must be performed on earth?

Jesus, was the great exemplar in this regard when He submitted Himself to John the Baptist to be baptized (see topic on baptism).

Now, if a man could be baptized after his death, he could sin with impunity while in the flesh, and then be washed clean while in the spirit world, without any effort on his part to accept or reject the Lord in the flesh. And the mortal probationary period would be fruitless. The prophet Alma declared, *"This life is the time for men to prepare to meet God"* (Book of Mormon, Alma 34:32).

But how does a man who accepts the gospel in the "Spirit World" get baptized? The answer is the Priesthood. The Priesthood has, *"the power to seal on earth, and whatsoever is sealed on earth is also sealed in Heaven"* (Matthew 18:18).

Through these Priesthood sealing powers, as contained in the Melchizedek Priesthood, people who have died without the privilege of being baptized while in mortality, can be baptized vicariously by proxies. That is to say, men in the flesh can be and are baptized for the dead by the Priesthood, a power that has no earthly limitations.

The doctrine of baptism for the dead is not new or original with the Latter Day Saints.

Like other truths of the restored gospel the principle of baptism for the dead was practiced by the Saints in the Meridian of Time. The Apostle Paul made reference to this practice while trying to convince the Saints at Corinth of the literalness of the resurrection. *"Else what shall they do which are baptized for the dead, if the dead rise not at all? Why are they then baptized for the dead"* (1 Corinthians 15:29)? In other words *"if you don't believe in the resurrection why are you doing baptisms for the dead"?*

It is apparent from the nature of Paul's argument for the resurrection, that the Saints in the Meridian of Time were involved in baptisms for the dead. So also do the Latter day Saints do baptisms, and sealing for the dead in the many Temples the Lord has caused to be built for that purpose.

How merciful, indeed, is the Lord who has provided the way for every man to have the opportunity of receiving the Gospel of Jesus Christ, whether in the flesh or not.

Can a man procrastinate the day of his repentance until he enters the spirit world and then repent and be saved in the Kingdom of Heaven? The answer is a resounding, no! He will have no greater incentive in the spirit world to accept Christ and repent than he did in mortality. Because the belief systems we learn in mortality go with us to the spirit world.

Death does not wipe our memories clean, neither does it deny us our agency.

There is a division that occurs when we die. Lets call it a partial judgment. All spirits, upon mortal death, enter into a confinement area called the spirit world. Those who have been just and valiant in the testimony of Christ enter into a place of rest known as Paradise, within this spirit world. While those who have not heard the Gospel and those who have heard it and rejected it, are not privileged to enter Paradise.

While on earth those who have not been valiant in the gospel or who have rejected it, while in the flesh, mingle with those who support their viewpoints and also those who do not. Those who will argue for the Church and those who argue against it. However in the spirit world they are no longer co-mingled with those who believe, as we are in mortality. This separation makes a change of heart more difficult, as kindred spirits tend to fortify one another just as we do in the flesh. To die, as a mortal, and then wake up in the spirit world does not, automatically, eradicate or change ones belief system.

Those who have never heard the Gospel message and receive it from missionaries in the spirit world, and who accept the efforts of loved ones or friends on earth, and are baptized vicariously, by the authority of the priesthood, move to the place of *"rest"* in Paradise (see Book of Mormon, Alma 40:12). Here they await the resurrection and final judgment, at which time they will be, *"judged according to men in the flesh"* (D/C 138: 32-34).

And where do the missionaries come from in the spirit world? They come from the spirits residing in the place of rest or paradise (see Doctrine & Covenants 138: 57).

The spirits that do not qualify, in mortality, for the area of "Paradise", and who must remain in the spirit prison can not leave their area. Their condition is clearly illustrated in Luke 16:19-31.

In these scriptures provided by Luke, the Savior gave us the parable of the rich man and Lazarus, and clearly points out that the wicked, in this case the rich man, could not come to Paradise where Lazarus was because of a fixed gulf. That makes sense doesn't it . . . . a prison, after all is a prison. A place of confinement. The only way anyone can enter the Paradise part of the Spirit World, is to accept the gospel, and repent of their sins, and be baptized, by proxie, by the authority of the Melchezidek Priesthood.

When Jesus died on the cross He, as a spirit, was very busy as we read in 1 Peter 3:18-19, *"By which also* (by His spirit) *he went and preached unto the spirits in prison"*. Jesus bridged the gap or gulf so that the unbelieving and disobedient spirits could be preached too . . . . and only then and because of this "bridge" could vicarious work for the dead be done.

Vicarious work for the dead as practiced by the Mormons, is truly a labor of love. Mortal men and women perform saving ordinances, by proxies, for their kindred dead to provide departed loved ones with the opportunity of salvation.

Baptisms performed in behalf of spirits need not be accepted by those spirits unless or until they so desire and are ready for them. Remember in the spirit world we still have agency. Mortal Saints engaged in this work are virtual saviors to their kindred dead, in that they perform a service for them that they cannot do for themselves.

The Latter Day Saints build temples in which to perform sealing ordinances, eternal marriages, and baptism for the dead, all of which are designed to establish bonds, ties, and covenants that extend beyond the realm of mortality and earth life into the eternities.

Take it from one who knows . . . . temple ordinances performed in behalf of departed loved ones . . . . are balm for the soul.

The object of this great effort for our kindred dead is to identify and establish by patriarchal order, for each family, an unbroken link from Adam to the latest born.

This program is of such vast importance as to be a threat to the existence of this earth, if it is not accomplished or in good process at the time of the second coming of the Lord.

Jehovah declared to Malachi, the Prophet, *"Behold, I will send you Elijah the Prophet before the coming of the great and dreadful day of the Lord: And he shall turn the hearts of the fathers to the children, and the hearts of the children to their fathers, lest I come and smite the earth with a curse"* (see Malachi 4:5-6).

Elijah did come and restored the keys or Priesthood authority, of the work for the dead to the Prophet Joseph Smith, April 3, 1836 in the Kirtland, Ohio Temple as recorded in the Doctrine & Covenants 110: 13-15.

The Lord in His infinite mercy, has provided a way for all men to have equal opportunity to exercise their free agency and accept or reject the Gospel of Jesus Christ, which is the divinely appointed way, or law to Eternal Life and Salvation.

Each man and women determines by the laws they live in mortality, what their ultimate status will be in the final judgment.

The predominate concept of divine judgment in Christianity today is the *"Heaven—Hell"*, viewpoint. This concept describes a judgment with a dividing line and two sides. One side is for good people and the other for bad. There are no allowances for in between. You either qualify for heaven or hell.

This view point is essentially correct but only as it applies to the destination of spirits when we die and go to the spirit world, to that area within the spirit world, that we are entitled to. However this partial judgment as discussed above separates those who are worthy of Paradise in the Spirit world from those who are worthy of hell or spirit prison, in the spirit world.

Eventually all men will enter the spirit world where we will wait for the resurrection and the final judgment . . . . a judgment that will consign us forever to a degree of glory . . . . the degree we have earned by the life we lived in mortality.

Some judgments are rendered by God while people are still in the flesh due to great and pervasive wickedness. Consider for example the destruction of the world population by flood, when only Noah and his family were spared. Or consider the judgment rendered by God on the great plains cities of Sodom and Gomorrah, when He rained down fire from Heaven, as referenced in the chapter on works. Or as recorded in the book of Mormon, 3 Nephi 9, which records the destruction of six cities by fire, four cities by flood, and six by earthquake, and all inhabitants, thereof because of gross wickedness.

These were judgments that resulted in many souls being removed from the earth and put in the spirit prison . . . . hell. But these actions by the Lord are not the "final judgment" which will occur after the resurrection of each of us.

Our divine parent is bending His every effort to qualify each and every soul for the best possible gift, that of Eternal Life. Eternal Life meaning to live forever in His presence as opposed to Eternal Death which is to live forever being denied His presence because of unworthiness. As He expressed through modern day Prophets, *"For behold, this is my work and my glory, to bring to pass the immortality and eternal life of man"* (Pearl of Great Price, Moses 1:39).

All souls good, bad, or indifferent will live forever and have awareness and presence of mind. This condition is the free gift given to all men as spoken of by John, (see John 5:28-29), specifically the resurrection. However, the point in question in the final judgment is not if we will live, but rather where and under what circumstances will we spend our eternal lives?

Our Heavenly Father's plan of salvation provides a *"mansion"* for every soul. Paul speaking of the resurrection to the Corinthians spoke of *"degrees of glory"*. *"There are also celestial bodies, and bodies terrestrial: but the glory of the celestial is one and the glory of the terrestrial is another. There is one glory of the sun, and another glory of the moon, and another glory of the stars: for one star differeth from another star in glory. So also is the resurrection of the dead. It is sown in corruption* (the corruption of the flesh*); it is raised in incorruption"* (the physical beauty of an immortal being) (1Corenthians 15:20-42).

People do not think and act the same, everyone is different and the Lord has decreed that all shall be judged and rewarded in accordance with individual effort and response to the laws of the gospel of Jesus Christ. *"And behold, I come quickly and my reward is with me, to give every man according as his work shall be"* (Revelations 22:12).

And again, *"And I saw the dead, small and great, stand before God; and the books were opened; and another book was opened, which is the book of life: and the dead were judged out of those things which were written in the books, according to their works"* (Revelations 20:12).

The Latter Day Saints believe that at the time of final judgment all mankind will be consigned to one of three degrees of glory. These degrees in descending order are; the Celestial, like unto the sun in glory, the Terrestrial like unto the moon in glory, and the Telestial, like unto the stars in glory.

The Lord revealed to the Prophet Joseph Smith considerable detail pertaining to the degrees of glory which are highlighted as follows (see Doctrine & Covenants 76:50-110):

Celestial (like unto the sun in glory)

Those who are worthy to inherit this degree of glory are they who have accepted and been valiant in the testimony of Jesus. These shall dwell in the presence of God and His Christ forever. All things are theirs, whether life or death or things present or things to come. These are they who shall inherit the earth. These are also they who received the gospel in the spirit world and would have received it in the flesh had they had the opportunity.

Terrestrial (like unto the moon in glory)

Those who inherit this degree of glory are they who are not valiant in the testimony of Jesus. These are they who were honorable men of the earth blinded by the craftiness of men. These are they who were spirits in the spirit prison who received not the testimony of Jesus in the flesh whom the Son visited and preached the gospel to, that they might be judged according to men in the flesh. Jesus administers to these in the Terrestrial Kingdom, and in the millennial world, where they receive of the presence of the Son but not of the fullness of the Father.

Telestial (like unto the stars in glory)

These are they who are murders, liars, adulterers, whoremongers, thieves, etc. They receive not the testimony of Jesus. Their numbers are reported as being as numerous as the sands of the seashore or as the stars in the firmament. These are they who suffer the wrath of God on the earth.

The moral law that each of us lives in mortality determines the character or personality that will prevail as our individual identity throughout eternity and consequently our final judgment destination.

For example those who faithfully follow the gospel of Jesus Christ will live a Celestial law in the flesh. Over time any other kind of behavior becomes foreign to their nature.

The same is equally true of the laws unique to a Terrestrial law of order. Those who live this law are known as honorable men and women of the world. They have rejected the sacrifices required to qualify for the Celestial world but are basically good people and live decent lives.

Those who live Telestial law in the flesh are wholly given over to materialism and self gratification. This lower law of behavior is typical to the world in which we now live.

These judgments of God are infinitely fair and merciful. Consider, for example the plight of a murder who would find no more comfort and peace in the Celestial Kingdom than he would in a congregation of Saints on earth. He would be out of his element and therefore very uncomfortable. He will inherit a *"mansion"* in the Telestial Kingdom.

I personally believe that these three Kingdoms, which are Kingdoms of glory, will be beautiful beyond our imagination.

But alas, I submit that, all will not be peace and joy in the eternal lives of those who inherit the Terrestrial and Telestial Kingdoms. In the final judgment the minds of these people will be "quickened", the record of Heaven will be opened (See Pearl of great price, Moses 6:61). I presume that means that we will have full recollection of our entire life as spirits, before we came to mortality. Everyone's "book of life", our memory, will be opened (See Rev 20:12) and we will then be able to compare what we achieved in our pre-existence, as spirits, with what we achieved in mortality.

In this way each and every person will have the power to judge themselves. All will have understanding of the entire plan of the Lord and the glory that could be theirs.

Some will rejoice and many . . . . most . . . . will be ashamed (Matt 7:13-14).

"As I live saith the Lord, every knee shall bow to me, and every tongue shall confess to God. So then every one of us shall give account of himself to god" (Romans 14:11-12, see also Philippians 2: 10-11). At final judgment we will all report our mortal stewardship to our God.

The knowledge those individuals possess, that permits this confession, will be of little value to the wicked and they will gnash their teeth and wail in the exquisite pain of regret.

Just as Satan and his followers do today. Because they know what their, eventual, eternal status will be.

Those who inherit the two lower degrees of glory will, I believe, experience regret that they did not seek out the Lord during their brief mortal life when they were given the chance.

There is no despair, no anguish, nor hopeless grief so terrible as the awful regret that what is done is done, and cannot be undone worlds without end.

What are fine landscapes, and land flowing with milk and honey, and such other beauties and comforts as the Telestial, and Terrestrial Kingdoms may afford to a soul burning in the unquenchable flame of deep and bitter regret.

Having said that, about the wicked, I hasten to also report that the Lord is anxious to forgive us if we but repent and turn altogether from our sins. Did He not perform the atonement for each of us? He suffered, more than we can imagine, in Gethsemane because we are so precious to Him. Also in the repentance process we come . . . . to be acquainted with the Lord, ... we come to know Him.

In point of fact the Lord is anxious to forgive us. (See Matthew 9:3-8, Mark 2:6-12 and Luke 5: 22-26).

In the repentance process we draw close to the Lord and in this closeness feel His magnanimity (being great of mind and heart), we feel of His patience, we feel of His joy for us . . . . of His long suffering. We get to know Him better. We begin to feel forgiven.

True repentance, acknowledging our unworthiness in the attitude of complete submissiveness on our hands and knees, begging for forgiveness . . . . is definitely worth the experience. In modern scripture the Lord declared, *"Verily I say unto you, notwithstanding [your] sins, my bowels are filled with compassion towards [you]. I will not utterly cast you off; and in the day of wrath I will remember mercy"* (See D/C 101:9).

The Lord is anxious to save. How anxious? Consider the great sacrifice He has made for each of us. Can we even begin to measure the width, the height or the depth of it? Is it even possible to plumb the measure of that atoning sacrifice of love?

The scriptures tell us *"that all man have sinned and fallen short of the mark"*.

Our own arrogance, and lack of humility is our biggest impediment to repentance. We typically refuse to acknowledge, to our selves, that we are sinners.

Not only does the joy and beauty of the Celestial Kingdom exceed all the rest but, I believe that, conditions and circumstances there are far different.

The Celestial degree of glory also has divisions. Many of the souls who qualify for the Celestial Kingdom do not qualify for exaltation in this kingdom, because they were not sealed to their spouses for time and for all eternity in the Temples of the Lord.

These souls will be angels or servants of those who inherit the highest division in the Celestial Kingdom known as *"exaltation"* (see Doctrine & Covenants 132:15-17).

Those who are worthy of and receive this highest degree in the Celestial Kingdom will be Gods and Goddesses. They alone will have family identity and retain the powers of procreation, a continuation of their seed (see Doctrine & Covenants 132:19-20).

They alone will qualify to inherit the earth which is to be celestialized after the millennium (see D/C 88: 25-26).

As is recorded in modern revelation; *"This earth, in its sanctified and immortal state, will be made like unto crystal and will be a Urim and Thummin to the inhabitants who dwell thereon, whereby all things pertaining to an inferior kingdom, or all kingdoms of a lower order, will be manifest to those who dwell on it; and this earth will be Christ's"* (Doctrine & Covenants 130:9).

From this revelation given to the Prophet Joseph Smith, we may understand that the earth will be changed from its present fashion and become an exceedingly beautiful and glorious planet.

Further the earth will be a Urim and Thummin which is an interpreter, or revealer. Which is to say, the inhabitants of the celestialized earth will be able to gaze into the earth and comprehend the manner by which it was created; the forces that govern its flight and its existence, and the same for all kingdoms of the same or lower order than the earth.

What a marvelous science lesson that will be, and it will all be true and taught by observation.

How surely will the inhabitants of the celestialized earth be Gods and Goddesses for they alone will know the secrets of creation. They will learn of the power by which Jesus commanded the heaving sea to be still, and the power by which He commanded the elements; and created the worlds (See Hebrews 1:1-3) and the water and all orders of life on the earth and all things thereon.

Those who qualify for the Terrestrial and Telestial Kingdoms will not be on this earth. I don't know where they will be but it won't be on this earth, whose destiny, we have just learned, is to be Celestialized.

And now we can plainly see the wisdom of God who sifts His children through a rigorous refining process in mortality; to make certain that only those of His children who put forth the effort to qualify will receive the great powers and blessings that He has in store for them.

Of a truth there is no place in the Kingdom of God for a rebellious, self willed, ungoverned personality.

With the vision of eternity before us who can say within themselves the treasures of the earth, here today, are of more value to me than the treasures of the Kingdom of God, whose reward is eternal. Will you serve God or Mammon, you cannot serve both, ... the choice is yours.